Unstaged Grief

MUSIC IN AMERICAN LIFE

For a list of books in the series, please see our website at www.press.uillinois.edu.

Unstaged Grief

Musicals and Mourning in Midcentury America

JAKE JOHNSON

UNIVERSITY OF
ILLINOIS PRESS
Urbana, Chicago, and Springfield

Financial support was provided from the General Fund of the
American Musicological Society and from the Office of the Vice
President for Research and Partnerships and the Office of the
Provost, University of Oklahoma.

Library of Congress Cataloging-in-Publication Data
Names: Johnson, Jake, 1984– author.
Title: Unstaged grief : musicals and mourning in midcentury
    America / Jake Johnson.
Description: Urbana : University of Illinois Press, 2025. | Series:
    Music
in American life | Includes bibliographical references and index.
Identifiers: LCCN 2024028958 (print) | LCCN 2024028959 (ebook) |
    ISBN 9780252046339 (cloth) | ISBN 9780252088407 (paperback) |
    ISBN 9780252047619 (ebook)
Subjects: LCSH: Musical films—United States—History and
    criticism. | Television musicals—United States—History and
    criticism. | Motion pictures—United States—History—20th
    century. | Television programs—United States—History—20th
    century. | Motion pictures—Social aspects—United States. |
    Television programs—Social aspects—United States. | Grief
Classification: LCC PN1995.9.M86 J64 2025 (print) | LCC
    PN1995.9.M86 (ebook) | DDC 791.43/6578—dc23/eng/20240710
LC record available at https://lccn.loc.gov/2024028958
LC ebook record available at https://lccn.loc.gov/2024028959

For Sandra Sue Romberg Johnson
For Bettye Lou Hiltibidal Smith

Mammy and Meemaw to me

Also when they shall be afraid of that which is high, and fears shall be in the way, and the almond tree shall flourish, and the grasshopper shall be a burden, and desire shall fail: because man goeth to his long home, and the mourners go about the streets . . .

—Ecclesiastes 12:5

Contents

How to Process This Book

The surface, or skin, of the Apollo Lunar Module was only 0.012 inches thick. Only as thick as a few sheets of aluminum foil. The skin had to be thin so that the astronauts could navigate the practically nonexistent atmosphere of the moon. For the men aboard, this thin skin was the only boundary between what might be and what in an instant would never be again, and yet somehow it was enough to take them to a faraway world and back home again. Imagine, there is so little behind the skin but empty, magical, and overwhelmingly deep space.

Now imagine a path flanked by large screens—movie screens, all playing moments from musicals written for an audience sitting not before a stage but a screen. Musicals, all without stages. Unstaged musicals.

Walking along this path shows the musicals as their writers hoped they would be seen. The camera lens determined for us decades ago what each of these musicals is or is not. Glancing behind or to the side of the path, however, you can see that the surfaces of the screens are paper-thin. These screens are propped up with two-by-fours, like the facades of dusty desert towns in old Westerns. What the audience sees might look like a saloon, but actors push through the swinging doors into another life, breaking character, not whiskey glasses. And yet somehow these screens are enough to take us and them to a faraway world and back home again. Imagine, there is so little behind the screen but empty, magical, and overwhelmingly deep space.

Surfaces, screens, and skins are the rocket fuel in this story, as I'll soon explain, and as this opening gambit demonstrates, surfaces can also be folded and bent into new shapes. By now, America in the 1960s has become another of those bending surfaces. Nothing happened in those years that can't or hasn't or won't be presented as a flat sheet, thin as foil, wrapping national memory like leftovers in the fridge. Thinkers during this era tried to develop ways of getting beneath these surfaces; Gilbert Ryle in 1968 argued that we ought to engage in "thick description" of cultural moments, while, later, Roland Barthes famously upheld the "punctum" as a prick beneath photographs to see what scratches out—yet surfaces remain an inevitable problem.[1] It's how we manage surfaces that makes all the difference.

I began this book as an extension of my previous work on the American musical, a genre whose intersections with unfamiliar places and values has been for me a wondrously parted curtain into the American psyche. My first books on musical theater center on belonging and belief; this project extends and aligns the two. As with belief and belongingness, grief is an interconnected and complex network of experiences, feelings, practices, and performances. Yet unlike belief and belongingness, grief has a reckoning. Not everyone can be promised a life of belief or belonging, but none will be spared grief. The shared experience of sadness, even more than the longing for acceptance or for something beyond this life, makes this the most entangled project I've attempted to unravel.

To my way of thinking, belief, belonging, and grief are essential and overlapping pathways toward community and betterment in America; *Unstaged Grief* rounds out my trilogy examining the American musical's role in shaping that path ahead. I am committed to telling stories about shared musical experiences and am particularly drawn to examples where those shared encounters do not at first appear to be shared as I enjoy showing how in those moments listeners experience togetherness, something bigger than themselves, and, in a word, feel *enchantment* because of it.

This book is amassed of many key interactions, places, people, ideas, and an innate curiosity for building enchanting stories. *Unstaged Grief* developed alongside *The Possibility Machine: Music and Myth in Las Vegas*, a volume of essays I also compiled for the University of Illinois Press. Beneath both books is a curiosity for what makes America work the way it does. In Las Vegas, I sense a machinery of dreams and possibility where just about any new world is possible because we believe that, in fact, Las Vegas has that very special quality. The task in *Unstaged Grief* is to attend to how the possibility inherent with musicals disguises big feelings when worlds come to a close.

Portions of chapters 1 and 4 were written as this book came into focus. Other versions appear in *The Oxford Handbook of the Television Musical*, edited by Raymond Knapp and Jessica Sternfeld, and in *The Cambridge Companion to Rodgers and Hammerstein*, edited by William Everett. Although I had no plans to write about grief when I began working on those projects, it was because of those opportunities that I began to sense the broader story through which you are about to journey. Stages are important to my argument; it's fitting that you sense the various stages this book went through too.

I wish to thank my editor, Laurie Matheson, for taking on projects that increasingly push the envelope. Also, thanks to Gary Smith and Tad Ringo and others at the University of Illinois Press for taking care of me and these books so well over the last several years. Mathew Campbell beautifully engraved all of my musical examples, willingly leaning into the creativity of the project, which just wouldn't have been the same without his handiwork. I was lucky to be joined by colleagues and friends over the last few years as we converted some chapters into lecture performances. Not only were these terrifically fun and energizing, but they also helped me refine parts of my thinking. Heaps of thanks to Jeremy Small, Autumn West, and Davy Green for their musicianship and friendship and generous, kind spirits.

My students and colleagues and friends near and far are never far from my mind. Something about each of them is in this book—surfaces that stack and wrinkle and make the world pass differently. BrieAnn, Cora, and Magnolia are, as always, lingering in these pages as they are in my heart.

And to the two grandmothers whose leaving so soon is something I continue to grieve, I dedicate this book.Unstaged Grief

Unstaged Grief

Grief Hides

How to begin a book about endings.

Unstaged musicals of the 1960s are a medium for grief. Intended for screens rather than the stage, unstaged musicals feel both immediate and distant—close to audiences everywhere, yes, but further and further away from those live crowds that musicals seem intended to seduce. Whether screened in movie houses or broadcast through television into living rooms across America, screen musicals of this era capture the often-unspoken sadness of watching history steal away the world as it is and waiting in anticipation for whatever new beast was slouching toward Bethlehem to be born. They grieve the end of a world.

This grief is not always apparent, in part because musicals seem to have so little to say about grief. And what they *do* have to say about suffering or chaos or pain may appear to us on the whole as unhelpfully tidy. The musicals common to film and television of this time are often characterized as escapist fantasies, ebullient apologists for happy endings. Musicals show us how to keep grief at bay. Don't they?

Even as musicals defend against the kind of desperation common at the end of a world, they can't help but participate in a network of grief in America, for America, about America. My title speaks to this entanglement of screens and sadness. Grief has stages, the psychiatrist Elisabeth Kübler-Ross told the world in her landmark 1969 book, *On Death and Dying*: denial, anger, bargaining, depression, and acceptance.[1] Kübler-Ross's five stages of grief enter the scene at the precise moment the so-called Golden Age of musical theater—that is, an influential handful of decades defined by a cohesive style and story strategies and theatrical content, and not necessarily an indication of a *best* moment in musical theater (though some do make that very claim)—makes its exit.[2] These parallel moves feel significant to me. I am persuaded by how the engine of musical theater as built in the opening decades of the twentieth century begins to sputter just as a new language emerges to process what that engine was trying to outrun—in short, the grief for a world slipping away, whatever that idea might mean to people then and now.

A central conceit of this book is that grief hides. Like the monsters of our childhood imaginations lurking in closets, under beds, in dark corners everywhere, grief retains its power by withholding from the world. And withheld grief is a growing grief. My work is to follow a suspicion that unprocessed grief remains embedded in emblems of an era where a collective turmoil was powerful enough to close the door on one world and jettison us into another. Similar to the characters in Philip K. Dick's 1962 novel, *The Man in the High Castle*, whose trauma amid the Second World War transported them unknowingly into an alternate timeline of global winners and losers, I suspect America has failed to recognize and process the grief of this dynamic era. What world ended and what world began in those years is less intriguing to me than the grief implicit in those endings and beginnings. That is what I am trying to get to the bottom of here. And perhaps near the absolute bottom of the list of culprits where grief lays hiding would be the musicals specifically made for television and film. Musicals on screens are so unassuming in just about every way imaginable. Point taken. To be honest, if I were a monster called Grief, I'd hide behind a musical too.

And that's also what I mean here—the American musical is an unsuspecting, squeaky-clean surface that so cleverly holds back grief. The musical is a skin, a covering, a hide for deeper, darker, bigger feelings. Grief hides beneath musicals. We might cheekily call the catalog of musicals populating our cultural landscape, then, *grief hides*. "Bless your beautiful hide," the fur-trapping backwoodsman Adam Pontipee bellows in *Seven Brides for Seven Brothers* as he starts to imagine his ideal wife. The musical, too, is a beautiful hide. A beautiful, fun-loving, fiercely repressed grief hide.

Marshall McLuhan introduced the expression *the medium is the message* in his 1964 book, *Understanding Media*, a phrase that made McLuhan into a towering figure of his time and became the source of both his ridicule and praise for the rest of his life.[3] His statement is punchy but simple. The ways we send and receive information became in the twentieth century more important than the content those media presumably carry. A particular medium—say, a telephone—alters our expectations and limits or expands the field of possibility in a particular telephone-y way even before a word or message is conceived. Relay that same information over a telegram and, well, we now have a different message. As McLuhan put it, "The 'content' of any medium is always another medium," making every message a nesting doll of media inside of media inside of media.[4] The medium matters. The medium makes the message possible. The medium *is* the message.

This book considers the nesting dolls within musicals—a peculiar and particular genre (er, medium) that craftily withholds its messages from the world. I am writing here about musicals written expressly for film or television—musicals that first arrived *unstaged*, in my words—which, like any other media, emerge into the world already shaping the message they attempt to deliver. My attempt in these chapters is to rethink how the medium of unstaged musicals spreads a particular kind of message, the message we assume musicals of this kind are trying to deliver, at any rate, as a kind of refractive gaze into the distorted worlds of surface and depth that have accrued in the age of McLuhan and ever since. I am hoping in this book to dislodge from the medium of unstaged musicals the thing that sits at the very core of their message but that has yet to be fully heard: grief for a world that is ending.

I chose this era of the 1960s because it seemed to be so aware of its own capacity for dynamism. The 1960s saw tremendous social change, unbelievable technological advancements, tremendous violence, and an upheaval that continues to churn an unsettled stomach in American politics. It also witnessed the foreclosure of the so-called Golden Age of American musical theater. Andrew Lloyd Webber and Stephen Schwartz's rock musicals about a human Jesus and Stephen Sondheim's concept musicals about the disintegration of just about every institution held sacred to Americans were a sharp change from the worlds of Richard Rodgers and Oscar Hammerstein, or George and Ira Gershwin, or Alan J. Lerner and Frederick Loewe. It was Lerner and Loewe's 1960 Broadway hit *Camelot*, in fact, that was mythically grafted onto the legacy of the young progressive John F. Kennedy, who was stopped in his tracks on November 22, 1963. At that moment, whatever *Camelot* represented, and whatever Kennedy represented, stopped holding the master narrative.[5] Both seemed to pass out of this world around the same moment.

On the other end of my time span, screen musicals up to 1953 were common. Very common. Musicals never intended to be staged were churned out of Hollywood movie studios in large numbers. As technology bloomed and Hollywood became an equal player with Broadway, the unstaged musical became ubiquitous with this era. Probably no single year was more wildly successful on this front than 1954, which saw premieres of iconic screen musicals *White Christmas*, *Seven Brides for Seven Brothers*, *Brigadoon*, *A Star Is Born*, and *There's No Business Like Show Business*. For me, this rush of successful movie musicals marks a watershed moment, beyond which nothing was ever quite the same.

So the source of my story bends back to 1954 in order to mark when this tap starts turning off. The resultant drip of screen musicals populates the rest of this book. I am compelled by the absolute paradox of these musicals, their pervasiveness in the waning moments of this era, and the abrupt change they signal for how Americans understood themselves. In examining musicals mostly between the years 1954 and 1968, this book nominates the "age of great dreams," as David Farber called the 1960s, as one that wants to teach us strategies for coming to terms with how even the greatest of dreams must come to an end.[6]

Denial, anger, bargaining, depression, and acceptance: by now these stages seem universally applied to any number of reasons for grieving, including the loss of a pet, a career, a missed opportunity, or leaving a religion behind. Grief and its various stages, Kübler-Ross later refined, are not limited simply to death. Nor are they linear. Grief manifests in messy ways and in as many orders. Any time a world ends, grief is messily there.

Each of my five chapters loosely corresponds with one of Kübler-Ross's stages. Her mechanism for grief has given me an imperfect structure to work with and against, which means at times highlighting the singularity of a particular stage of grieving and at other times allowing other facets of grief to show. While in each chapter one unstaged musical pulls focus to one stage of grief, true to my approach, these chapters tease and slide in and out of order throughout, and their relationship to their given stage of grief should not be taken as absolute. Grief spills and so do these studies.

Chapter 1 focuses on Stephen Sondheim's television musical *Evening Primrose*, a rare, curious horror story about mannequins and humans.

Sondheim's story also forecasts a form of denial. The way characters and values in this musical hide away in the face of the unutterable terrors of the world barely catches by the tail the worries and isolation of actual worlds poised to crumble and burn. The second chapter sees in *Seven Brides for Seven Brothers* evidence of anger as men tried and failed to return from the Korean War to the same America they left. On offer in this chapter is how Americans come to terms with an unsettling responsibility for creating and then destroying their own monsters. Chapter 3 turns to the musical *The Singing Nun*. This musical, concerned with the imperfect balance of conflicting value systems, resonates with an intense desire for bargaining—with God, for God, against God—in order to somehow not choose one over the other. The fourth chapter, on the 1962 remake of *State Fair*, pulls back the gossamer and thin lace of rural nostalgia and sees the musical engaged in a deeply philosophical and existential question: What sadness awaits us when we get everything we want? Constantly skirting depression, characters in *State Fair* emblemize a concern for the unmet wish and attempt to name the heaviness of purposelessness weighing down modern communities. Chapter 5 then orbits acceptance, Kübler-Ross's final stage of the grieving process, on the wings of *Chitty Chitty Bang Bang*. This unlikely likeable musical about enchanted cars, lonely fathers, and the shaky line between who we are and what we might become drops hints from above that flighty dreams of a new world must, at some point, land on the ground. The book's brief conclusion extends Kübler-Ross's fascination with hope through some forecasts of what kind of work musicals seem to be doing for a world skittish about (and desperate for) hope.

I chose this framing in part because Kübler-Ross's book appears at the tail end of this era. Something about her work feels pulled through the beginning of this long decade, a specter haunting its earliest moments, trying to be made known but lacking the vocabulary. *Unstaged Grief* tracks in some part how that vocabulary gets built through—and gets built into— unstaged musicals. Whatever the world we grieve, musicals grieve it too.

One purpose of this book is to rethink the boundaries of our imagination, both about grief and musicals of the 1960s but also about the way ideas swerve in and out of American consciousness. Because grief so often and so successfully hides in musicals of this era, my approach in *Unstaged Grief* is to foreground the connection that screen musicals share with other icons of popular culture. I primarily do this by reading images and texts against one another, disrupting the surface that images naturally privilege in order to reveal the depth within and beneath. I borrow strategies from art historians on this front and, tinkering with other tools soldered and salvaged from disciplines here and there, concoct a methodology of deep analyses and graphic readings of musical excerpts to reveal what musicals on screens are trying, but often don't know how, to say about grief.

Attentive to the fact that grief traces unique paths for individuals and that grief so very often attends to us in loneliness, I nonetheless navigate some claims for how communities struggle to identify and process grief.[7] I'm interested in exploring how screen musicals align with and jostle apart our collective sense of how we move through, away from, and out of these various stages of grief. I'm no less interested in how worlds end. And I'm especially interested in how acceptance of endings can offer clarity on new beginnings.

My strategy for upholding *Unstaged Grief*, then, is to source its ideas almost entirely from the milieu of the 1960s. Occasionally I will direct the reader's attention to more recent or developing conversations in the academic world—but only occasionally. Although my citational practice here is on the whole divested of current scholarly debates, I hope that will not be enough to conclude that I am unaware of them. It is simply not my goal with this project to reinscribe an extensive bibliography.

The thought partners I enlist reflect my deliberate effort to engage the era head-on without the burden of clearer vistas or entrenched discourse that come with afterthought. Marshall McLuhan's work is central here, but so, too, is that of C. S. Lewis, Susan Sontag, Arthur C. Danto, Ray Bradbury, and Roland Barthes. Visual artists of the time whose styles are often labeled as quintessentially American, such as Edward Hopper, Norman Rockwell, Andy Warhol, and Andrew Wyeth, interlace here as well, to say nothing of musicals or magazine covers, newsreels, novels, poems, philosophies, and films and television from the era. My approach here, in fact, is both a nod to and an experiment in McLuhan's assertion that the electronic age thrust the world into a galaxy of surfaces all related yet seemingly isolated—what he called *the global village* and what we generally refer to as a postmodern age seemingly populated only with surfaces.[8] This book's interplay between embodiment and perception—depth and surface—is at an extreme; musicals in any ordinary way must in some fashion betray their liveness, their unmediated values. Musicals designed expressly for screens lose that impulse (though maybe not always its conventions) and so strike me as an odd way of managing what is essentially a new medium of surfaces where, as this book attests, grief and emblems of grief frequently hide. What this book holds together, then, is a fascination with disturbed surfaces. The grainy, silty bottom of an American grief swirls to the surface in this disruption. My feeling is that only then can grief be seen, be known, and finally be allowed to teach us its lessons.

All of these references thread together throughout this book, coming in and out of the texture as chapters develop. I want to introduce them to you here now, since they are in many ways my squad—a gaggle of characters whose arc and development are worth paying attention to as chapters move past. But they also are a binding braid for this story. Many characters, like Hopper and Rockwell, offer important commentary on decline and ends as their own realist styles become eclipsed in this era not just by abstract expressionism and other modernist movements but also, as Arthur C. Danto argues, by the advent of a philosophical worldview that insists *anything goes*.[9] These voices are important corollaries to my own interest in unstaged musicals. Not only are they additional witnesses to the last gasps of a world before it ends, but their iconic status even today as emblems of Americana run parallel to Golden Age musicals. I choose here to place their images and perspectives into conversation with unstaged musicals, and I choose here to buttress such images with contemporaneous thinkers. These swirls of ideas twist the thread that binds our story together.

Musicals built for the screen are an ideal study for this phenomenon. They forfeit the kind of spatial depth, of embodiment, of dimension, that is otherwise a given attribute of the genre of musical theater. These unstaged musicals turn in a way not unlike the reels pedaled by the Man in the High Castle—dangerous and subversive because they show the world as it could be, not as it actually is. I am not all that interested in crossing my eyes to see dimensions behind the surfaces of these images, but I am interested in disturbing their rest by constantly layering, gathering, stacking, and bundling these flat surfaces in company with other flat surfaces. In our own age of surface, where the very idea of depth is held in tremendous suspicion, perhaps this is the only recourse remaining. What I value is releasing what for so long has been held captive and misunderstood and taken for granted. Amid debates of surface and depth, grief has survived our inattention to what really is lurking beneath: what we will not see because we may not be able to bear the consequences of looking.

But look we must, even if the conclusions we draw from looking are only provisional. Phenomenologist Gaston Bachelard said as much in his 1958 *The Poetics of Space*. "To verify images kills them," he claimed, "and it is always more enriching to imagine than to experience."[10] *Unstaged Grief* is written with imagination of heart and mind. It plots meandering routes and weird shortcuts on a familiar map of our cultural landscape to better catch a view of how art participates in collective expressions and experiences that might not be so obvious. As an age of vast and lasting conspiracies, the 1960s seem to be a fitting era to investigate a shared experience. I guess you could say this book is its own conspiracy theory. In my view, musicals and grief and belonging and belief are all conspiracies—literally, *con-spired*, as in things we breathe in and out together—and I'll try in these pages to reorient exactly how grief manages our world as it passes through and among us like a virus.[11]

What I am trying to get at, and what may help to know at the outset, is that this book is a meditation on historical writing, cut more from poetry than from prose. A poem is "a made thing" in Greek (*poiesis*) which is also a beautiful name to give something we labor against—I made a poetic phrase, perhaps, but it is also true that the poetry has made something of me in the process of writing it. The same feels true for this book. I confess that I approached this project not as a scholar of art but as an artist whose medium is scholarship, a reframing of traditional academic labor that I believe the project requires and is bettered by. Old maps are of limited use here. The spill and spread of ideas in this book occupy an immense and wild territory that I had to learn how to navigate using unusual and unproven tools and that you, in turn, are invited to pick up and handle and make a thing from yourself.

That's not to say that this book doesn't have familiar academic trappings or that in choosing art I am abandoning scholarly rigor. A reframing is not a wholesale rejection. In these pages I experiment with a practice of persuasion cast from correlation rather than causation. Correlation sees patterns, gathers them together, and considers what can be made of this creation. Correlation lingers at the level of question, which is where possibility remains greatest, and gives the creative mind a chance to make worlds before the intellect annihilates them. Precisely because it sees an incomplete picture of the world, then, correlation offers a valuable way of thinking that cannot so readily be cashed into an economy of conclusion, answer, fact, or other metrics of scholarly marketplaces. What I hope readers take from this practice is an invigorated way of thinking and writing about and listening to that which resists our attention. Grief puts up a fight, but so do habits, scholarly or otherwise, that can so often take more than they give to the world.

And that's really the point I want to be clearest about as I leave you for our story: grief is a collective experience. The musicals I have selected for this story are a little like nails on the back of our nation's door, supporting loose and discarded coats from the harshest world outside. And the 1960s were quite an age of harsh worlds—witness to the inescapable violence of one world ending and another trying yet unable to be born. It is up to each of us to determine how the end of one world might be celebrated or loathed. That said, I suspect none can admit that neither cheers nor sneers are enough to quiet the turbulence of never knowing what world, precisely, is readying to be born in its place. If there was ever a time when unstaged musicals of the midcentury mattered, that time may be now, at the end of the world as we once believed it to be.

FIRST STAGE

Denial and Isolation

One of our patients described a long and expensive ritual, as she called it, to support her denial. She was convinced that the X-rays were "mixed up"; she asked for reassurance that her pathology report could not possibly be back so soon and that another patient's report must have been marked with her name. When none of this could be confirmed, she quickly asked to leave the hospital, looking for another physician in the vain hope "to get a better explanation for my troubles."

—Kübler-Ross, *On Death and Dying*, 34

Frozen Figures

Stephen Sondheim's television musical *Evening Primrose* follows a community of social nihilists who live in a department store by night and hide in plain sight as mannequins by day. It's a fantastical and colorful story about a simple and common impulse: to deny the world we grieve. The show aired only once, on November 16, 1966, for decades kept alive thanks to meandering bootleg copies and ardent fans who borrowed the show's songs for the cabaret circuit and revues. With a run time of fifty minutes and consisting of merely four songs, it remains an unsettled musical—like its characters, caught within the gambit of looking one way and yet behaving another. "The music sneaks into *Evening Primrose*" is how Robynn Stilwell puts it.[1]

By the time *Evening Primrose* snuck into the world, American musical theater was being decentered by television just as the American family was increasingly centering itself around it. Between 1960 and 1965, television viewing time in the average American home increased by twenty-three minutes per day, all while radio, film, and theater audiences declined.[2] The television musical was one attempt to redirect the public's attention to the theater. *Evening Primrose* was the latest of a relatively new genre of television musical and was programmed as part of *ABC Stage 67*—ABC's ultimately unsuccessful attempt to extend the anthology series of the 1950s, which included musicals written by Rodgers and Hammerstein, Cole Porter, Jerry Bock and Sheldon Harnick, and Jerry Adler, among others, siphoned onto the small screen. As John Bush Jones describes the times, "People didn't have to go to Broadway; Broadway was coming to them."[3] And in this case, it came to them in their very living rooms. Sneaky indeed.

This change of scenery seems to have been part of Sondheim's thinking all along. "What I wanted to do was find ways of using television . . . [to] write a musical that could not be done on stage," he explained.[4] To be sure, his turn to television has been historicized as pragmatic—book writer James Goldman needed rent money and saw in *ABC Stage 67* an opportunity for quick cash. Perhaps equally as decisive was Sondheim's determination to find success in a new medium after *Anyone Can Whistle*'s notorious failure on Broadway in 1964. In any case, *Evening Primrose* remains a Sondheimian novelty, his only musical written for a medium other than live theater. After collaborating on Broadway versions of Elizabethan romance (*West Side Story*, 1957) and ancient farce (*A Funny Thing Happened on the Way to the Forum*, 1962), Sondheim's shift of focus to the televised macabre of *Evening Primrose* entered unannounced, was received as unremarkable, and remains mostly unexplained.

As unexpected as it may be, this one hour of television not only fits importantly within Sondheim's evolving theatrical sensibilities, but it also captures the terrors of another time. A box in the living room was becoming more and more the norm by 1966, as were frozen TV dinners and the decentered American family life. Even more, though, times were uncertain; it had been a mere four years since the Cuban missile crisis had brought the United States to the brink of nuclear war, and less than three years after Abraham Zapruder's black-and-white footage of Kennedy's assassination had been piped onto these same screens in American homes. Sondheim's audience was already on edge, and television was the vehicle through which this anxiety had been most persistently rendered since the 1950s.

It seems a strange choice on Sondheim's part, then, to use television— which by the mid-1960s featured a wonderland of variety shows with quick and easy laughs, *escapism* in a word—to broadcast a musical whose serious sensibilities were decidedly of the previous decade. Like the grotesque mannequins in *Evening Primrose*, the show seems to be modeling a fashion out of place with the times its audience lived in and more in line with a world the audiences anticipated and grieved. This chapter tells a story about the fear and petrification implicit in denial—being stopped cold, feeling helpless, knowing nothing can be done. Also on the table here is a case where the musical feels in denial too. It is up to us to decode, unravel, and pull into focus the message this musical contains that it didn't even know it was carrying.

In 1955 *Life* magazine published a story on the nuclear testing done outside Las Vegas, Nevada. At the center of the story was how the bombs were detonated near a village of department store mannequins, who were studied afterward as if they were proxies for actual humans. The accompanying photographs and description of the aftermath of these test explosions must have stopped readers cold:

> A day after the 44th nuclear test explosion in the U.S. rent the still Nevada air, observers cautiously inspected department store mannequins which were poised disheveled but still haughty on the sand in the homes of Yucca Flat. The figures were residents of an entire million-dollar village built to test the effects of an atomic blast on everything from houses to clothes to canned soup.
>   The condition of the figures—one charred, another only scorched, another almost untouched—showed that the blast, equivalent to 35,000 tons of TNT, was discriminating in its effects. As one phase of the atomic test, the village and figures help guide civil defense planning—and make clear that even amid atomic holocaust careful planning could save lives.[5]

The photographic vividness of nuclear-weary, immobilized humanoids is a fitting image to represent the era; as Richard Falk put it in 1971, "The great danger of an apocalyptic argument is that to the extent it persuades, it also immobilizes."[6] The level of detail inscribed onto the mannequins for the sole purpose of being blown up is curiously unnerving—some mannequins were dressed in formal attire, others were staged doing everyday activities: playing cards, sleeping, and even watching television. The mannequins' appearances after the blast were horrifying. Singed arms, scalps, and pant legs littered the ground, while torsos, held upright by poles driven into the ground, leaned from the blast force. Through it all, the placid faces kept smiling—what looks like price tags hanging from their necks like a toe tag in a morgue. Coupled with their slightly reclined bodies and oddly cocked heads, these finely dressed mannequins stand at once as tragic and comic, decidedly out of place within a desert landscape as devoid of flora and fauna as the plastic faces were of life.

Deploying mannequins outside the realm of a typical department store refocused and defamiliarized the very material culture that was at the heart of the Cold War. If an entire village of mannequins masqueraded as

FIGURE 1.1 Mannequins after atomic test blast in Nevada. *Life* magazine, May 16, 1955.

an actual middle-class community, it should be no wonder that thoughts of the inverse began to emerge. In these images, viewers witnessed the striking disturbance of effigies created in their own likenesses populating a simulated war zone, not in some distant land but on American soil.

A similar interpretation can be constructed from Edward Hopper's 1960 painting *People in the Sun*. Like those in the *Life* photographs five years earlier, Hopper's subjects, too, seem out of place in their environment, over-dressed and seated in the direct sun. With their chair legs mimicking the triangular shape of the distant mountains, four of the seated figures stare blankly into the landscape, reclined in a stance similar to those Nevada mannequins, post-blast. Given that Las Vegas casinos during this time marketed nearby atomic test blasts for tourists, even hosting watch parties quenched by specially made atomic cocktails, Hopper's figures seem to match the absurdities of the time, reflecting a moment when Americans were prepared, poised even, to play with fire.

These frozen figures embody the scenario in Marlen Haushofer's 1963 novel, *Die Wand* (The Wall), in which an invisible wall suddenly and without explanation surrounds a woman on vacation in the Austrian countryside. The only people the woman can see on the other side of the wall are lifeless yet upright—frozen in place as apparent victims of some kind of attack. Though this wall contains the untitled character within its

FIGURE 1.2 Edward Hopper, *People in the Sun*, 1960.

limited domain, it also acts as a protection from whatever force petrified all humans outside of it. Haushofer's story extends the image of immobilizing fear that preoccupied Hopper and others during this time.

I'll return to Hopper's figures in the sun a little later. But first we might also usefully consider some thematic similarities with a 1961 episode of *The Twilight Zone* called "The After Hours." Rod Serling here tells the story of Marsha White, who, after becoming trapped in a department store at night, is greeted by store mannequins and reminded that her preordained month in the human world is over and that she must now return to her true self as a mannequin. At first Marsha is terrified, but realizing that she had simply forgotten, she eventually concedes, noting that her time among the humans was "ever so much fun." The episode's parting shot is a close-up of a mannequin, an exact likeness of Marsha, on display in the department store the following morning. The camera pans wide as Serling narrates: "Marsha White, in her normal and natural state a wooden lady with a painted face, who one month out of the year takes on the characteristics of someone as normal and as flesh and blood as you and I. But it makes you wonder, doesn't it? Just how normal are we? Just who are the people we nod our hellos to as we pass on the street?"[7] In an age of increasingly sophisticated technological espionage, it was one thing to distrust those strangers among you, as manifest in such films of that era as *The Thing from Another World* (1951) and *Invasion of the Body Snatchers* (1956), and quite another to fear that your true self—your "normal and natural state"—is not what you believed it to be.

Across enemy lines similar fears were also given expression. In 1961, the same year that our *Twilight Zone* episode about Marsha White was broadcast into American homes, Russian scientists launched two successful space orbits of an unmanned vessel. What made these flights remarkable is that a mannequin was seated in the cockpit. Ivan Ivanovich, as he was named, was made to look as close to human as possible. His face, in particular, was given eyes, eyebrows, and eyelashes. He so resembled a true human that scientists placed a placard on Ivan's spacesuit that read "dummy" to forestall someone finding and trying to capture, resuscitate, or gain intelligence from Ivan when he returned to Earth. These true-to-form likenesses troubled even those working closely with Ivan. As one advisor to the Soviet's cosmonaut program remarked, "There really is something deathly unpleasant in the mannequin sitting in front of us. Probably it is not good to make a nonhuman so much like a human being."[8]

What makes this story all the more alarming is that Ivan's hollow orbiting body was actually teeming with life, filled with dozens of white and black mice, guinea pigs, reptiles, bacteria, and human cancer cells, along with a collection of scientific tools used to measure the effects of space on a human-like body. Creating a humanoid for the purpose of carrying life within itself falls on uneasy minds even today. Freud's concept of the *unheimlich*, or "uncanny," continues to haunt modern perceptions of the strangely familiar; as humanoids and humanoid voices increasingly permeate all facets of industry, education, politics, and entertainment, their not-quite-humanness creates an "uncanny valley" of affective alienation.[9] Imagine, then, the scene when Ivan parachuted to Earth, a visitor from the sky landing in an unsuspecting Russian village. The villagers were reportedly so alarmed at the sudden intrusion of space-race paranoia into their lives that they angrily punched Ivan in the face, taking him to be a Western spy.[10] If human imaginations were capable of giving a mannequin human features, they were also led to vent their frustrations and fears with a punch in that dumb, plastic face. For these villagers, as for their American counterparts, mannequins and their dark purposes were becoming altogether too real.

Adapted from John Collier's enigmatic short story from 1951, *Evening Primrose* tells the tale of Charles Snell, a disgruntled and struggling poet who becomes so disillusioned with life in New York City that he chooses to escape it, to live free of troubles, by secretly living within a department store. Like the mollusk that shares his name (*Snell* sounds like *snail*), Charles is a creature of comfort who finds it natural to retreat inward in the face of perceived threats elsewhere. A self-exile to a department store—a temple of excess and modern conveniences—is hardly the heroic act he thinks it to be.

So we meet Charles in a rush of movement, but quickly we see he is only seeking to stay exactly where and as he was. He is grieving a world at end. But he wants to build a new one by recreating the old one. Charles is an echo of Douglas in Ray Bradbury's 1957 autobiographical novel *Dandelion Wine*.

> "I'm alive," said Douglas, "but what's the use?
> They're more alive than me. How come? How come?"
> And standing alone, he knew the answer,
> staring down at his motionless feet.[11]

EXAMPLE 1.1 Undulating accompaniment and unsettled chromaticism populate Charles's opening song, "If You Can Find Me, I'm Here." Music and lyrics by Stephen Sondheim.

After the store closes and the shoppers leave for home, Charles comes out of hiding and sings the musical's opening number, "If You Can Find Me, I'm Here."

The song starts as a metered bit of poetry, underscored lightly by a two-note pulse like a heartbeat, before erupting into a wild circus waltz. Charles's vocal line crawls chromatically. It rubs and flits against a rapid orchestral groove that at once accelerates his ascending melody while also darting its eyes like it belongs somewhere else. His music is worldly in a way. Charles is a part of the Beat Generation, after all, and the assurances of department store life, plush with comforts he readily accepts, cuts awkwardly against his metric of authenticity that measures consumption

EXAMPLE 1.2 Endings of "If You Can Find Me, I'm Here" from *Evening Primrose* (left) and "I'm Still Here" from *Follies* (right). Music and lyrics by Stephen Sondheim.

as evidence of American emptiness. Charles's opening number is jagged and itchy in its new skin. It actually goes nowhere. The music teaches us a truth: our protagonist is in denial.

His final rush of melodic invention spills out in the repeated phrase "I am here," drawn across a leaping minor seventh. Four years later, Sondheim uses a near-identical ending to aging and former showgirl Carlotta Campion's torch song "I'm Still Here" in *Follies*. Charles and Carlotta declare their arrival at two very different stages in their lives—Charles as a victorious rebirth into a new world and Carlotta as a badge of surviving the world as it is. Enwrapping both Charles and Carlotta into the minor seventh leap—a wild and desperate musical gesture, by the way, that feels thrown like steaming pasta noodles against a wall—wrinkles their fates toward each other.

The song stops abruptly as the night watchman comes near. Singing full-throated draws a certain attention, it turns out. Charles quickly poses as a mannequin, which convinces the watchman but awakens a nearby mannequin, who is actually a real person who has been in character, presumably, all day. "Not too bad for a beginner," the mannequin tells Charles. Both mannequins melt back into life like Narnian creatures lifted from the frozen spell of the Ice Witch.

Charles is surprised to discover that there are lots of other people living in the department store, too, who at various times were similarly disenchanted with the outside world. Always avoiding the store's night watchman—who, by the way, seems like a simulacrum for the grief they are all so clearly hoping to outrun—the others quickly assess Charles as a non-threat to their insular world and adopt him into their nocturnal community. Charles soon meets and falls in love with Ella (as in Cinderella), who, as a six-year-old, was accidentally left in the department store one evening by her mother, found by the others, and enslaved ever since to their leader, the boorish dowager Mrs. Monday.

In the musical production, Sondheim clearly wanted to capitalize on the television medium. One scene in particular stands out as being nearly impossible to transfer into any live setting. During the song "When,"

Charles and Ella's growing attraction is revealed only to the audience through interior monologues voiced over by the actors—the others in the scene observe only the couple's silence—all done while Charles distractedly plays a hand of bridge with Mrs. Monday and some of the others. As in Samuel Barber's one-act opera *A Hand of Bridge* from 1959, Sondheim here mixes the game's banter with interior monologues from both Charles and Ella. The scene is both clever (with Charles playing the *dummy* hand at times) and effective, offering an advance glimpse of the couple's stiff demise: Sondheim's displaced voices, suggesting ventriloquism, foreshadow the duo's dummy-like state as embalmed lovers. But even more,

FIGURE 1.3 Top: Anthony Perkins as Norman Bates in *Psycho* (1960). Bottom: Anthony Perkins as Charles Snell in *Evening Primrose* (1966).

Charles, Ella, and these other poser mannequins closely resemble here the scene of desert mannequins likewise seated playing cards, cheerlessly awaiting their atomic annihilation.

Director Paul Bogart recalls that the scene was constructed as a voice-over from the beginning, but he was dissatisfied with the outcome. "I didn't like being on their faces while they were thinking," he admits. "I'd do that differently now. I'd have them sing just outright, and the other actors would just not hear 'em. On Broadway, you can get away with that."[12] The scene, according to Bogart, would then appear not unlike what can be done with stage magic today, although the vocal and camera effects required for the number led Stilwell to call it "one of the most striking televisual musical numbers of the era."[13] For Sondheim, then, television offered a medium through which to explore musical theater in a much more intimate way than in staged productions.

Now, there's something else uncanny happening here. Anthony Perkins, who played Charles, was a close friend of Sondheim—the two eventually cowrote the screenplay for the 1972 mystery thriller *The Last of Sheila*—and reportedly was handpicked for the role by Sondheim himself. Although Perkins had appeared in a number of films and Broadway productions, he was by then most instantly recognizable as the schizophrenic murderer Norman Bates in Alfred Hitchcock's *Psycho* (1960), where Perkins's character is an amateur bird taxidermist spending his days making dead things

EXAMPLE 1.3 The sneaky, nervous accompaniment to Charles Snell (top) is the broken-up accompaniment to the world that composer Bernard Herrmann created for Norman Bates in the 1960 film *Psycho* (bottom).

FIGURE 1.4 Top: Charmian Carr as Liesl von Trapp dancing with Daniel Truhitte as Rolfe Gruber in *The Sound of Music* (1965). Bottom: Charmian Carr as Ella Harkins lounges with Anthony Perkins as Charles Snell in *Evening Primrose* (1966).

seem real and confusing his true self with his mother's persona, which he affixes to himself like a glass eye. In *Evening Primrose*, audiences are asked to shake that image of Norman Bates and find in Perkins a relatable and lovable Charles Snell—a poet who, like Bates, nonetheless prefers a life among taxidermic creatures to the world outside his cloistered space. In retrospect, even Charles's busy theme music huddles around the same cluster of pitches Bernard Herrmann conjures for Norman Bates in *Psycho*'s infamous murder scene. What Herrmann terrorizes by stacked pitches Sondheim teases out through an endless loop.

On the other hand, Charmian Carr, who plays Ella, had instant recognizability of a different sort, since she had played the role of the most famous sixteen-year-old in musical theater, Liesl von Trapp, in the 1965 film production of *The Sound of Music*. Television audiences might easily recount the famous gazebo scene in that film, where Liesl waltzes with and dreams of growing up in the arms of Rolfe, the teetering telegram deliverer with Nazi loyalties. Later in the film, Rolfe's politics come between the two lovers, and the politically exiled von Trapp family narrowly escapes Nazi forces when Rolfe finds the family hiding and attempts to turn them in.

Persona and character become two sides of the same coin in the mintage of the theatrical. Perhaps viewers had anguished only one year earlier over Liesl's close encounter with Rolfe's murderous ideology. To then see the same actor fall into the arms of another untrustworthy young man, familiar to some audiences as a murderous psychotic, must have been dizzying.

The situation brings to mind another horror icon of this era, Boris Karloff, whose image and voice were nearly inseparable from his enigmatic role as Frankenstein's monster. In parallel to Boris Karloff's voicing of the Grinch in *How the Grinch Stole Christmas*, which would air one month after *Evening Primrose* on rival CBS, Perkins carries residue of the monster into this role of an endearing (and singing!) poet. That both Perkins's and Karloff's sexualities have been watched with suspicion may also matter here. If only subliminally for most 1966 television audiences, their roles as "monsters turned nice" flatten peculiarly American anxieties over communists and queers into a single concern, left over from the pink and red scares of the 1950s. Within the span of a single month, both Perkins and Karloff enact the villainy of difference for television audiences, slipping into the uncanny valley of the near human just far enough to perform their different versions of the queer redemption narrative.

Evening Primrose's themes of petrification echo what were for audiences in the 1960s likely familiar themes of frustration, anxiety, and mistrust. Amid increasing anxieties of the nuclear age, consumerism became the balm of the times, though not without consequence. In *The Minimal Self*, historian Christopher Lasch characterizes American culture of the postwar era, with its fixation on mass consumption, as narcissistic, with consumers increasingly viewing "the world as a mirror, more particularly as a projection of one's own fears and desires."[14] "Narcissism," he continues, "signifies a loss of selfhood, not self-assertion. It refers to a self threatened with disintegration and by a sense of inner emptiness."[15]

Because the ideological conflict between Soviet and American powers centered on the issue of capital, mannequins, as literal models of commerce, were familiar embodiments of American ideals. And, in parallel to Ivan's artificial womb for life, mannequins in America were vehicles for another way of living: consumerism. Charles's escape into a temple of material goods feels as American as apple pie.

Perhaps on equal footing with consumerism, though, was the strong pull of objects toward nostalgia. The department store and the museum are twinned impulses, one making a way of life possible and the other making a way of life memorable. Both look backward, not forward. This comes across clearly in Norman Rockwell's cover painting of the November 3, 1962, issue of the *Saturday Evening Post*. The image, titled *Midnight Snack*, is meant to be comic. We see an aging night watchman of a museum seated on the pedestal hosting a life-size horse and armor, the horse mounted by a full suit of knight's armor. Other suits of armor stand upright all around him, watching guard over the guard. Only the horse's side eye gives the story its drama—watching the watchman in perfect stillness.

The scene takes place in the Higgins Armory Museum in Worcester, Massachusetts, founded by steel magnate John Woodman Higgins in 1931 as a projection of his love for medieval lore. Higgins died in October 1961. Rockwell may have had the founder's death in mind when designing this cover. The watchman himself seems ghostly, drawn into the spooky and dark world where empty suits of armor spring to life. If the watchman is Higgins, then, like the watchman in *Evening Primrose*, he has to be avoided

The Saturday Evening POST

November 3, 1962 · 20c

Eichmann And His Trial
By His Prosecutor
The Attorney General of Israel

A Short Story by William Saroyan

Memoirs of a Monster By Boris Karloff	California Feud L.A. vs. S.F.	'Genius' at Green Bay Fullback Jim Taylor

FIGURE 1.5 Top: Cover of the November 3, 1962, issue of the *Saturday Evening Post*, featuring Norman Rockwell's *Midnight Snack*. Bottom: Charles posing near a supposed mannequin in *Evening Primrose*.

EXAMPLE 1.4 Excerpt from "I Remember." Music and lyrics by Stephen Sondheim.

at all costs or the game is up. The midnight hour, the spooked props, and the collision of life where it does not belong all add up to make *Midnight Snack* a similar equation pondered by *Evening Primrose*. Department store mannequins uphold denial in the face of nuclear annihilation while the armory museum displays bygone technologies of protection. Neither seems to allow space for dealing with the cataclysm.

Those materialist aspirations, however, are quickly overturned when Ella sings to Charles of her memories from a childhood outside the department store. Remember, she was left there accidentally as a child. Her inability to describe the outside world without relating it back to the material goods surrounding her makes her life among products pitiable and empty. She grieves the world she left and wants to return to with all her heart. With his back to the camera for the entire scene, Charles appears frozen in place as Ella sings, "I remember snow / Soft as feathers, / Sharp as thumbtacks, / Coming down like lint, / And it made you squint / When the wind would blow." The childlike wonder of the scene bleeds into morbidity in the final moments of the song, however, as the unsullied memories that Ella uses to recall the world she knew only as a child gives way to a more sober realization that "the bluest ink / Isn't really sky." "And sometimes I think," she winces, "I would gladly die / For a day of sky."

Ella perhaps serves as a caution against materialist impulses and the failure to distinguish copy from original. She has spent a life in a confused place where humans pose as inanimate things and relationships with commodities take the place of lived experiences. She knows the world is more, but she can't help her metaphors. Her melodic gestures are mostly triads—simple, childlike even, reaching out to the world beyond the department store—but ultimately, she is bound by her vocabulary; only the words about the inside world land with any tonal finality. She needs to escape

FIGURE 1.6 Edward Hopper, *New York Office*, 1962.

her world, but so does Charles. They both seem incapable of discerning which of their worlds is real and which is the one merely standing in for the other, which also means they do not know how to grieve which world will be lost when choosing the other.

These themes suggest a registered paranoia among both Americans and Soviets in a time of an increased and burdened notion of opposing forces: isolation and globalization. Military weaponry whittled down the globe's immense geography into mere minutes as the threat of annihilation loomed overhead. At the same time, fascinations with imposter humans led to a cultural spin on the meaning of aliveness when faced with the possibility of sudden disaster.

Which is why I want to return now to Hopper's painting *People in the Sun*. The realism of Hopper's image harshly depicts the cool frenzy of petrified observers, perhaps silently awaiting the whir of an oncoming missile. The title itself, *People in the Sun*, radiates an energy of radioactivity as the figures wait patiently for instant death. Only the book reader, the most animated of the five subjects, positions himself at a disadvantage to the awaiting destruction, immersed within his open book. The seated reader is an archetype in Hopper's work, alluding to what Ivo Kranzfelder claims is the "demise of public life under the tyranny of intimacy."[16] Some of Hopper's other work—for example, *Hotel by the Railroad* (1952) and *Chair Car* (1965)—capture gatherings of frozen loneliness. *New York Office* (1962) is particularly notable in this context. The woman appears to be holding and reading a telegram, yet her position within the lighted store window gives her the impression of a store mannequin. In *People in the Sun*, the seated reader is darkened by the shadows of those in front of him, part of an opposition that erupts between light and shadow, explicitly connected to mobility and petrification.

Hopper's shadowed reader also hints at the well-known philosophical tale in Plato's *Republic*. Once shackled and forced to face dancing shadows along a cave wall, Plato's prisoner escapes the cave only to encounter the sun, for the first time seeing that the reality that had been constructed for him is only an illusion. Rather than going about his life outside the cave, he returns to his fellow petrified prisoners and tries, in vain, to convince them of the falsity of their world and, among other things, the extraordinariness of the sun. Hopper's reader, then, reveals an inverted interpretation of Plato's story, one in which by seeking escape from the blinding sun he edges closer to the shadows cast before him.

Likewise, Charles—a poet, another man of letters—chooses asylum from the grating pace of reality, favoring the darkened department store and eschewing the light of the outside world. In the Cold War context, Charles's retreat into the department store seems very much like a retreat into a bomb shelter—both spaces voluptuously well-stocked with provisions to satisfy anyone's needs and desires while hunkered down in the aftermath of a nuclear attack.

It is Ella who convinces Charles to return to the world of light or, as she puts it in song, to "move her to the sun." Both Ella and Charles want to escape their reality, yet we hear within "Take Me to the World" the confused state of the world that awaits them. The stakes are highest for Ella. Even if she and Charles were to stay together in the department store, Ella would remain in bondage to Mrs. Monday. On the other hand, Charles is comfortable where he is. His poetic talent is appreciated in the underworld, and he clearly understands that a poet's stock is quite low in the world he has escaped.

The scene that unfolds as a duet anticipates the scene in Sondheim's *Into the Woods* (1987) between the witch and her daughter, Rapunzel.

EXAMPLE 1.5 Comparing Charles's pleas for Ella to "stay with me" (top) with those of the Witch to Rapunzel in "Stay with Me" from *Into the Woods* (bottom). Music and lyrics by Stephen Sondheim.

The relationships here are in some ways parallel. Rapunzel and Ella are young, blonde, and naïve, and both have been held in bondage most of their lives. The witch and Charles are poets (we are introduced to both of them through a Sondheimian version of rap) who are wizened to and afraid of the outside world—conceptualized as the world beyond a department store in one story and the world awaiting beyond the woods in the other. When Charles objects to Ella's plans for escape, he continually pleads for her to "stay with me," carving the same melodic shape that the witch does as she begs Rapunzel to stay with her. Their melodies are wide and stretchy, leaving plenty of space between the notes. Their arguments likewise leave much to the imagination. The witch and Charles can promise worlds of abundance, comfort, and predictability, but their assurances can extend only so far to those who haven't had the chance to see for themselves how they might live in a new world: Plato's allegory in toto. Ultimately, Charles aborts his plan to stay in the department store when Ella asks if he loves her. "I love you more than poetry," he offers as he quickly announces plans for their escape that night.

The witch loses everything when Rapunzel chooses to leave. So does Rapunzel, who is crushed by a giant. Charles and Ella fare no better. Despite their plans to move into a new world, Charles and Ella do not escape the department store, making it only as far as the storefront window. Their plan is discovered by Mrs. Monday, who calls for the help of the Dark Men, who live in the neighboring undertaker's store. The Dark Men intercept and kill Charles, Ella, and take out the night watchman, too, using the undertaker's tools to transform their bodies into wax mannequins. In the final scene, passersby ogle a new window display featuring a set of bride, groom, and minister mannequins in the exact likeness of Charles, Ella, and the night watchman. Mrs. Monday and the Dark Men succeed in burying the secret of the underworld department store hideaway; moreover, they do so by burying the couple in full view of the daylight they sought. The entire scene is underscored by a reprise of Charles and Ella singing "Take Me to the World." In a dark turn of affairs, Charles does indeed move Ella to the sun.

In a nod to the macabre tone of his television musical, Sondheim admits the difficulties and limitations inherent in the genre itself:

> Once [film production] is done, it's done. It's embalmed and that's the problem. The great thing about movies and television movies is you can make them perfect and they're always there. And the terrible thing is you can make them perfect and they're always there. They cannot be changed. They're not alive and if you make a mistake that's also always there.[17]

The permanency of the film or television medium can certainly seem disadvantageous and troubling to someone who cut his teeth in live theater. Still, if the television musical was not Sondheim's genre, he had yet to hit his stride on Broadway, even if he much preferred the flexibility and communicative properties of live theater. For him, live theater involved "two-way knowledge," demonstrating an aliveness that was palpable, even inherent, in the experience. "A movie doesn't know you're alive," he once said. "Theatre does."[18]

Given that Sondheim's reputation runs perpendicular to the sensibilities of the so-called Golden Age—wholeness, reconciliation, or just plain cockeyed optimism—the frequent backward-looking glances of his musicals indicate that the midcentury provided a useful foil for him to work against. Sondheim here seems late to the game; by the mid-1960s, audiences were interested less in television as a medium for reality than as a purveyor of easy entertainment. *Evening Primrose* may in fact have seemed the musical-theater equivalent to a government public service announcement, reminding viewers to take precautions to ensure survival. Duck and cover and all that. Perhaps for this and other, less benign reasons, *Evening Primrose* remains a largely obscure piece of television theater.

But the gist of the story here is about surrender in the face of unspeakable news. A television musical haunted and horrified by the world outside gives ample evidence that denial fails, that running from grief and hiding from grief fails, and that even a fantastical genre like musical theater fails to imagine a way around the problem. The sadness here is thick, the cart broken down, and a musical, of all things, the medium and the message. Small wonder the world felt stopped in its tracks. Frozen. "No one ever told me about the *laziness* of grief," C. S. Lewis admitted, frozen in loneliness and grief after the death of his wife.[19]

The musical's title is a reference to the *Oenothera biennis*, the common evening primrose that flowers triumphantly and spectacularly only as night falls. Fitting, don't you think? Past their postures frozen in fear, complacence, or indifference, this musical piped into American homes just as the darkest moment descended, to aid in denying their worst fears and to help them believe again in a sunlit world where they, too, can feel alive.

SECOND STAGE

Anger

This patient makes sure that he is not forgotten. He will raise his voice, he will make demands, he will complain and ask to be given attention, perhaps as the last loud cry, "I am alive, don't forget that. You can hear my voice, I am not dead yet!"

—Kübler-Ross, *On Death and Dying*, 46

CHAPTER 2

Sobbin' Men

Set in 1850 in Oregon Territory, *Seven Brides for Seven Brothers* (1954) tells the story of a backwoods family of seven handsome brothers at odds with the nearby townspeople. Adam Pontipee, the oldest, marries a woman named Milly from this town and brings her home to the farm filled with messy, backward, and lonely brothers. Milly's loving but exhausting work taking care of the men's messes eventually leads the other six brothers to seek out wives of their own—first by courting and, when that fails, by stealing other women from the town.

What follows is Gene de Paul and Johnny Mercer's musical adaptation of Stephen Vincent Benét's 1937 short story "Sobbin Women," itself a modernized and colloquially spelled take on the Roman legend Rape of the Sabine Women. In all versions of the story, the hostages eventually fall in love with their captors. After 1974 the world knew this phenomenon as Stockholm syndrome. In 1954 it was simply the plot point in a cheery musical about sad men and the women who help make their world right.

There is a lot of surface area to this story. Benét's tale of seven unkept backwoodsmen softened by the care of a young woman is considerably similar to the Disney animated film *Snow White and the Seven Dwarfs*, which also premiered in 1937. At the surface level, the two sets of brothers are setups for comedy. Both Disney's dwarfs and the Pontipee brothers are named using a gimmick—personality traits like Grumpy and Sleepy for the dwarfs, all names beginning with *H* in Benét's story, and in the 1954 version the brothers are (with one exception, comically) named alphabetically from the Bible.

Beneath the fun surface there is something more, of course. Both stories are also about mirrors. Both stories see the women involved as pure, snowy, frozen. Both stories are about isolation, loneliness, jealousy, and doing whatever it takes to keep the anger from boiling over the kettle.

This chapter sees *Seven Brides for Seven Brothers*, which premiered, almost to the day, one year after the Korean Armistice Agreement, as a story centering on the grief of rehabilitation. The brothers are wild and unkept, prone to violence, and unwelcome among the townsmen. They have a hard time relating to women, eventually resorting to a reconnaissance mission to capture them from the enemy. What I suggest is that the brothers sing and dance as haunted emblems of America's so-called Forgotten War, struggling to move forward with their lives. When pulled through the slovenly fabric of World War II and the subsequent Korean conflict, the story of loving the unlovable and forgiving the unforgivable threads sympathies away from the captive women and toward the thieving men. This is a story, then, not of sobbin' women but of sobbin' men: men who grieve the consequences of survival.

There is a scene in *Seven Brides for Seven Brothers* that tries to deflect grief by naming it out loud. It takes place in the middle of the film. The Pontipee brothers are lovesick and depressed. They had met girls in town during a barn raising, but despite being taught manners and proper courting techniques by their sister-in-law, Milly, seemingly dashed their chances with them after a brawl with several local townsmen. Their inability to fully repatriate into the town's codes of conduct sets the brothers apart. They were lonely and their world moved slowly because of it.

In their loneliness and grief, the brothers sing "Lonesome Polecat" while slowly performing what must be daily chores for backwoodsmen—chopping and sawing wood for the fire. It is an inverted work song. The rhythms of farm labor hardly match pitch to the rhythms of this sluggish dirge. Their movements are burdened, slow, near motionless in the winter snow, seized by a sadness.

The brothers are positioned sharply against the white snow, making the entire scene of six frozen figures a mirror of what may be the saddest scene of any film musical of this era, the moment in *Meet Me in St. Louis* (1944) where Margaret O'Brien's character, six-year-old Tootie, smashes the six snowmen she had helped build after learning that the family will be moving to New York City after the holidays. Her older sister, Esther, played by Judy Garland, kneels in the snow across from O'Brien, a reflection of grief between them and a graveyard of broken, frozen figures all around. James Agee's review of this scene in *Meet Me in St. Louis* failed to find the same meaning. "These statues were embarrassingly handicapped

FIGURE 2.1 Top: Margaret O'Brien and Judy Garland across from one another in a graveyard of six frozen snowmen in *Meet Me in St. Louis* (1944). Bottom: Six Pontipee brothers do chores while singing "Lonesome Polecat," figures frozen in their grief in *Seven Brides for Seven Brothers* (1954).

from their birth, and couldn't even reach you deeply by falling apart," he writes.[1] He actually finds the cast itself to be more fixed than the snow-men—too "perfectly waxen" as he puts it.[2]

These dual scenes of six frozen figures falling apart in front of us are a glimpse beneath the surface, a picked wound, a barometer of what lies beneath. *Meet Me in St. Louis* was a decade old by the time *Seven Brides for Seven Brothers* premiered in theaters, but the two screen musicals speak past each other as the end blurs in front of them. The winter before *Meet Me in St. Louis* premiered, an American B-24 was shot out of the air by German artillery and crashed into a small French village, killing a family in their home and all ten men aboard the plane. The B-24 was named *The Lonesome Polecat*. Now, that name might more easily register with audiences in 1954 as the Native American character in the comic series *Lil' Abner* (made into a Broadway musical one year later by *Seven Brides*'s writing team of Gene de Paul and Johnny Mercer and choreographer Michael Kidd) than as some homage to a lost plane of men in World War II.[3] But the surfaces wrinkle compellingly. When the Pontipee brothers name *themselves* lonesome polecats, their grief is not toward lost airmen or innocent civilians but instead a grief tethered to survival. The other side of victory was haunted. Even C. S. Lewis failed to make his magical Narnia a utopia in his 1950 *The Lion, the Witch, and the Wardrobe*. Whether by wardrobe or by a movie musical, the tools of escape left everyone out in the cold. Always winter, never Christmas.

What the song "Lonesome Polecat" offers is a point of departure from the heroic sadness amid World War II. The 1950s were by comparison less defined, a decade more committed to consumer obsessions, forced normalcy, and tackiness than to heroism. The grief of the age feels heavy. The "Forgotten War" leans like the brothers in the snow. If we are to understand the ruptured grief of broken snowmen and frosted woodsmen as different, we have to think of *Meet Me in St. Louis* as the end of something about America and *Seven Brides for Seven Brothers* as representing the beginning of something different about it, something angrier about it, something wholeheartedly heartbreaking about it. Nineteen fifty-four started America fresh. It wasn't entirely ready.

In Benét's original story, it was Milly's idea to steal the girls from town; once the girls are in tow, she plays the role of good cop, punishing the brothers loudly while secretly teaching them how to woo their captives.

In the musical, Milly is only indirectly responsible for the kidnapping. She uses her influence initially to get the brothers cleaned up and teaches them proper ways of courting a girl. In the musical number "Goin' Co'tin'," Milly explains that you can't just grab a girl like a flapjack—you have to *court* her. She teaches them how to dance, which the brothers find they actually enjoy, and they practice channeling their anger toward the kind of song-and-dance productivity musicals value the most. This is also the first time the brothers sing—Milly's lesson in what is good for the town is likewise a lesson in what is good for a musical.

Milly takes the cleaned-up, mannerly brothers into town to help with a barn raising. The town girls notice the Pontipees immediately, but so do their suitors. What follows is one of the more iconic dance scenes in film musical history, a choreographed one-upping between the newly civilized Pontipees and the barbaric townsmen. The brothers are polite and mannerly with the girls. The townsmen don't buy it—they know the Pontipees are backward and during the barn raising try to rouse their true selves with sneak attacks. Chaos ensues soon enough. The newly built barn collapses with the tussle. Whatever new life the brothers were trying to build comes crashing down in an instant with the barn. There is no reconciliation here, no new structure big enough for both the outcasts and the accepted. The Pontipees leave for home broken. Soon after, they sing, frozen in the snow, of being lonesome polecats.

This failure to integrate into their surrounding community puts the Pontipees in company with musical theater villains, not heroes. The community of Claremore, Oklahoma, in Rodgers and Hammerstein's 1943 musical *Oklahoma!* failed to integrate the dirty, backward farmhand Jud Fry as one of their own. The community can only heal and find reckoning by getting rid of Jud; his death at the end of the show triggers a tidal wave of lyricism from the town. "I've got a beautiful feeling / Everything's going my way / Oh what a beautiful day," they all sing, Jud's body not yet cold in the ground.[4]

Oklahoma! and *Seven Brides for Seven Brothers* speak toward each other, not least because the film version of *Oklahoma!* arrived in 1955, one year after *Seven Brides for Seven Brothers*. Both are set in parts of the country not yet settled or even officially parts of America—Indian Territory for one and Oregon Territory for the other. Settling the frontier excuses behaviors in each of the shows, but the villainy of those behaviors is treated quite differently. Like the Pontipees, Jud lives on the outskirts of the town. Like the Pontipees, the threat he poses to the community is a specifically sexual one: muscular, entirely aggressive and repressed, Jud and the brothers are equally lit fuses as far as their neighbors are concerned. In his soliloquy "Lonely Room," Jud names his sadness of estrangement, from Laurey, yes, but also from the town. He commits through the song to act on his instincts to steal Laurey for himself. His song could just as easily be placed in the mouths of the six lonely Pontipee brothers, at this point in their film posed to act impulsively and steal girls for themselves.

> Goin' outside
> Git myself a bride
> Git me a womern to call
> My own

The final phrase's slow, sludgy climb through a D major scale shows just how ambitious a musical theater villain's humanity is to achieve. That Jud's assertive "my own" sags on the C sharp a half step away from resolution indicates that his soliloquy, no matter how humanizing it might hope to be, is at first a dream of acceptance but finally a nightmare of exclusion. Jud falls into company with operatic antiheroes of this era like Benjamin Britten's queered outcasts Peter Grimes or Billy Budd, and his eventual death feels haunted by Kurt Weill's judgment of pious and unfeeling community in *Street Scene* (1946).

But musicals of this era have a harder time with nuance and prefer not to ask what responsibility communities hold in making their monsters. "Lonely Room" was cut from the 1955 film, so audiences missed an

EXAMPLE 2.1 Closing bars of "Lonely Room" from *Oklahoma!* Music by Richard Rodgers and lyrics by Oscar Hammerstein II. Jud's stubborn scalar push to the top comes close but never quite finds resolution, leaving him out of tune with the others. The question seems to be whether Jud's C sharp or the community's sense of harmony needs to change.

opportunity to see or hear Jud's side of things. As a result, Jud dies in the film without the benefit of naming his loneliness. Jud dies a clear villain.

The Pontipees, despite carrying unlikeable and dark intentions similar to Jud's, are the heroes in their story. They are given voice to their grief. They are allowed to grieve their loneliness. Their loneliness, in fact, is what makes them heroes in waiting. The inability for the townspeople to recognize their role in making the brothers estranged and lonely turns the tables on the story and makes *them* the villains.

We next see the brothers moping in their old barn, essentially having given up. Adam comes up with the idea for stealing the girls after reading about the Rape of the Sabine Women in one of the two books Milly brought to their marriage: the Bible and Plutarch's *Parallel Lives*. With Milly's black book of Plutarch in hand, Adam is a vision of authority. He brings to mind images of the Bible-toting Reverend Billy Graham, whose celebrity status during the nation's revivalist movement of the 1950s made him a household name and his face a familiar sight. It was his face on the cover of *Time* magazine on October 25, 1954, pointing toward the viewer like Uncle Sam in the U.S. Army's recruitment posters ("I want you!")

FIGURE 2.2 Billy Graham on the cover of *Time* magazine, October 25, 1954—four months after the premiere of *Seven Brides for Seven Brothers*.

with a depiction of Eve's temptation behind him. Adam, her companion, is nowhere in sight.

Or is he? Graham's face is positioned opposite of Eve—her back to us, his facing forward, finger out and mouth caught in the shape of "you." Adam is all of us, the image seems to be saying. "When Adam, the federal head of the human race, sinned," Graham writes inside the magazine's pages, "we sinned with him."[5]

This gesture of inclusivity in Graham's face fills the frame with the audience. American audiences were by then accustomed to a sort of two-way mirror into the war effort, both religious and military. David Douglas Duncan's war photography from the earliest battles in Korea were published in 1951 as a "wordless" book titled *This Is War! A Photo-Narrative of the Korean War*—an early example of what in the coming decade would be called a coffee table book. Duncan allows his images of freezing soldiers, weeping soldiers, soldiers wounded, and soldiers walking stone-faced past bodies of fallen comrades to speak for themselves. In his brief introduction, Duncan implicated the viewer immediately, a literary equivalent to Graham's frozen face and pointed finger:

> Without you my book would be impossible. For *You* are deeply involved in this story. You are the Main Character. You are the one who survived— the one who lived to stand outside a crude aid station in the valley while awaiting word whether your comrades were still alive . . . or dead. You are the one who lived to sprawl loosely upon a city street while eating your can of beans. You are the one who didn't get hit, or freeze, or just disappear into the swirl of blinding snow when you and your comrades were surrounded by enemy troops in vastly superior force, then driven to the point of final exhaustion while marching out of the trap.[6]

Duncan later explains his photo-narrative approach, "wishing that it might have been possible to publish this book without a single written word so that the men might tell their own story," adding that he wanted "to present only a word screen upon which these men project their own story." Duncan's project resembles James Agee's 1941 *Let Us Now Praise Famous Men*, an ethnographic study of sharecroppers during the Depression. Agee also regrets that whatever will be made of the stories he tells, the hard lives he writes about will inevitably be betrayed by words. "If I could do no writing here at all, I would," he laments.[7]

Again, the scene with the brothers in the snow rushes in for explanation. They sing in metaphors, feeling lonesome as this, being mean as

EXAMPLE 2.2 Five-note sigh in "Lonesome Polecat." Music by Gene de Paul and lyrics by Johnny Mercer.

that. At the end of every verse, the metaphor runs out of steam and all that comes out is a weepy, five-pitched sigh. They are betrayed by their words. The best they can offer is a wordless account, an ancient pentatonic utterance of grief. Images of the Pontipee brothers caught in the snow, bundled against their grief, feel like an extension of Duncan's *This Is War!* project—*Seven Brides for Seven Brothers* becomes the screen Duncan was searching for to project the experiences of war that no words could ever describe.

Billy Graham visited servicemen in Korea during Christmas 1952, one year after Duncan's photos began circulating in America. On this so-called crusade, Graham comforted the dying and offered spiritual guidance for thousands of American troops. In the days leading up to Christmas, Graham delivered several open-air sermons. As recorded in his diary, which was published in 1953 as *I Saw Your Sons at War*, Graham's preaching led to mass conversions and commitments among men whose penitence and desire for acceptance made them weep: "When I gave the invitation, more than one-third of the men stood to their feet in front of their buddies to accept Jesus Christ as Saviour. Many were weeping unashamedly, men who had faced death just hours before; big, strong, tough Marines, weeping because of their sins and their need of a Saviour."[8]

When Adam picks up the black book to cheer the lonely and grief-stricken brothers—set during a winter presumably a century earlier—he appears as a charismatic leader, his wool-lined jacket drawing a straight line between him and images of Billy Graham preaching to weeping, weary servicemen. He launches into the song "Sobbin' Women," written in the style of a revivalist tune, and we are meant to perk up and listen closely.

Like "Sit Down You're Rocking the Boat" from *Guys and Dolls* (1955) or "Brotherhood of Man" from *How to Succeed in Business without Really Trying* (1961), "Sobbin' Women" participates in a growing trend within musical theater at midcentury, no doubt encouraged by the white gospel

movement and rockabilly aesthetic, to use a gospel musical style to moral-
ize a message of collaboration or spirited celebration. In these instances,
the musical narrowly escapes becoming a sermon. And even though these
film musical numbers rarely feature a Black character, Black sound nonetheless serves as a stand-in for spirituality.[9] Adam's improvisatory shouts
above the singing elevates the significance of the scene to a religious plane.
The brothers are taking matters into their own hands, taking back what
they feel is rightfully theirs. Adam is rousing a crusade.

It is in this scene when the brothers see themselves reflected in history.
They refer to themselves as Romans, of course, similarly eyeing the frontier
and building an empire, but they also compare their assault to Robin Hood
stealing from the rich in order to enrich themselves. "The victor gets all
the loot," Adam tells them. The loot, er, *women* in this song are weepy—a
clever collapsing of the brother's mispronunciation of Sabine and the act
of sobbing—but the song teaches the brothers that secretly these women
are thrilled to be part of the capture. "And though they'll be a sobbin' for
a while," they sing as they rush out to their wagons, "we're gonna make
them sobbin' women smile."

If Adam's spiritual revival collapses under the weight of Billy Graham
among Korean servicemen, the brothers' ensuing raid on the town traces
the edges of shame that many in the United States were feeling after the

FIGURE 2.3 Howard Keel as Adam Pontipee, singing "Sobbin' Women" to his
brothers.

raid on Short Creek, Arizona, on July 26, 1953. Short Creek was home to some 400 Mormon fundamentalists who practiced polygamy. An anonymous tip to the police claimed that the Short Creek community was plotting an insurrection. Led by Arizona governor John Howard Pyle, the state's National Guard stormed the compound just before dawn and took all but 6 into custody—including 263 children, most of whom were separated from their parents for over two years. Pyle had the law on his side but not public opinion. Perhaps because the raid took place only two days before the Korean Armistice Agreement was signed, initiating the return and repatriation of American POWs, Americans were largely shocked and dismayed by scenes of children being stolen away from their parents under the auspices of the American military. The Arizona Guardsmen were surprised to find no signs or evidence of any insurrection; instead, they found most of the community gathered together in the schoolhouse, singing.[10]

Seven Brides for Seven Brothers unwittingly enters into this conversation one year later but attempts to give their own nighttime raid and theft of other people's children a hint of religiosity and a heaping dose of good fun. The song's gospel framing feels like a crusade, a tune inserted into a foreign space to restore spirits, reclaim what was lost, and instill confidence in the righteousness of the quest. The resulting message is confused and mixed. We cheer for the boys because they are lonely and because we know the girls will turn their lives around, but mostly we cheer because they have made their point a moral one. On the other hand, we're talking about abduction and coercion. The brothers can get by with doing what Jud was killed for even thinking about.

But the scene works largely because of the work it does. The brothers have a mission, and that mission is to slow their sadness. To pull back into the world by angrily taking it back for themselves. And this mission seems largely acceptable, particularly when viewed through the lens of healing sobbin' men rather than protecting sobbin' women. Billy Graham said as much in the *Time* magazine issue with his face on the cover: "Oh, on the outside you put on a big front. You laugh and you joke and all the rest, but when you're alone, there it is—that void, that aching, that empty place. There is a questing; there is a hunger; there is a longing for something else in life; and you haven't found it yet and you want it."[11]

Once on the farm, the captured women live in the house while the brothers, punished by Milly and kept apart from the women out of midcentury propriety (the brothers in their haste forgot to kidnap the parson, so the women remain unmarried and pure), wait out the winter in the cold barn. The women are frequently pictured standing or sitting in front of a window. The brothers pass in and out of sight throughout the winter blizzards, going about their daily chores in sorrow while the women feel increasing stirs of cabin fever. "I think it's disgusting standing there where *they* can see you," says one of the girls to another, the piety of the town coming through in her voice. In some ways, the window out into the brother's world feels like a screen into a faraway world, like a projector into a wintery world elsewhere. Duncan's wartime images of soldiers huddled against the elements comes to mind—those at home left to stir and gawk and wait until the thaw. The women watch and wonder; the brothers can look back, but there is something between them.

Yet in other ways, the windows act as a frame of another sort—not one looking out but one looking in. Like a mirrored surface, the women in the windows appear distant and grotesque to the men. Windows and mirrors are, of course, operative indices. When a few of the brothers get into a fight with some townsmen early in the film, the youngest brother, Gideon, sees the action through the general store window. "Hey, it's us!" he excitedly tells the others before the fight comes crashing through the window—like Graham's pointed finger and Duncan's photographs a direct admission that what audiences see is both a mirror and a screen, a terrible reflection back as much as a horrifying window into the men's world. *Hey. It's us.*

We first get this woman-in-a-window moment between Adam and Milly on their wedding night. The true purpose of the marriage becomes clear to Milly almost immediately upon arriving at the farm: Adam has six brothers and she will be expected to cook, clean up after, and manage them like hired help. Milly angrily rejects Adam from their bed. Adam climbs out of the upstairs bedroom window and begins settling in for the night in a nearby tree. She comes to the window, directly across from Adam. The window separates Adam and Milly but also draws a line between two planes of existence: civility and godliness for Milly with ruggedness and individuality for Adam. They meet in the middle of those worlds with Milly's song, "When You're in Love," in which she explains that love makes you do many strange things, spills out in ways you can't always control, and that her anger in the moment was because, in truth, she had fallen instantly in love with Adam and wanted to build a life with him. The song softens the mood and Adam is invited back into the bedroom, but not

FIGURE 2.4 Gideon sees his brothers fighting through the store window. "Hey, it's us!" he yells, just before the fight comes crashing through the frame.

before falling into their bed and breaking it—a sign of lingering brokenness between them, a promise for greater dramatic cleavage to come.

Later in the film, Adam sings a reprise of "When You're in Love" not to Milly but to his lovesick brother Gideon. Milly, framed this time by the doorway, is there, however, seen overhearing the conversation. She has taught Adam what love means, but audiences never hear her join him in song. The original soundtrack includes an extended version of "When You're in Love" that was cut from the film. This extended version is an actual duet between Milly and Adam, their voices meeting in overlapping counterpoint. In the film, Adam and Milly sing the number separately, which makes the song a duet split in two, separated by something like a window. Reprises typically reunite or reinvigorate an idea stated earlier in the musical, accruing meaning along the way and, usually, resulting in a reconciled relationship. "When You're in Love" never quite accomplishes this, a signal that Adam and Milly have never fully accounted for their differences and that their union may remain unsettled in the eyes (and ears) of the audience.

Milly peering out the window toward Adam—and, later, the other women watching the brothers work outside from the window—makes the whole scenario feel unreal, as if these women are caught glimpsing through not just a window but a screen. Edward Hopper's paintings of women in windows from this era similarly rhyme with *Seven Brides for Seven Brothers*'s depictions of uncertainty and grief amid both war and wartime recovery. In *Cape Cod Morning* from 1950, Hopper shows a woman peering through an oriel window into the surrounding forest. We see her in

FIGURE 2.5 Edward Hopper, *Cape Cod Morning* (1950).

profile from a side window, framed by dark shutters and shadowed by the rising sun. The woman, like Milly, is wearing pink and has her hair pulled back. And like Milly, Hopper's woman peers through a window into the trees. Both women lean toward the outside world, the window a screen into something else, but what? To be feared? Hoped for? Two years later with *Morning Sun*, Hopper again depicts a woman in pink lost in thought staring out the window into the world. Women in windows and doors and mirrors seem in these stories to be locked in place, unsure of where or how to reach beyond the moment. The men are waiting on the other side, looking in.

Meanwhile, the six abducted women are holed up in the brothers' old room. It has been a long winter and they are unsure of how to feel. They are angry. They channel some of that anger toward one another. But they are also sad and lonely and channel some of those emotions toward the brothers. We learn that the women, having watched them through the windows for weeks, are more and more intrigued by their captors. They sing "June Bride" in celebration of a coming spring when Milly will give birth to her baby, a season they also hope will relieve them of boredom and sexual repression. Singing and posed in their white knickers, the six statuesque women are a negative print of the brothers outside in the white snow—whatever absence the men grieve, the women appear to be what might fill that space.

The image of the women likewise recalls Tootie's yard of anger-broken snowmen, but these women, despite being held captive against their will,

FIGURE 2.6 Milly sings "When You're in Love" to Adam on their wedding night, the window framing and separating the two.

are frozen in hope rather than in grief. The picture into the upstairs dreams of a young woman is similarly captured in Norman Rockwell's cover for the March 6, 1954, issue of *Saturday Evening Post*, which appeared while *Seven Brides for Seven Brothers* was wrapping up principal photography. *Girl at Mirror* shows a young girl sitting in front of a mirror in her white knickers. She is much younger than the six women in *Seven Brides for Seven Brothers*, but her posture and position in front of the mirror suggests

FIGURE 2.7 Top: The six captured women sing of their loneliness in the brothers' upstairs bedroom. Bottom: Norman Rockwell, *Girl at Mirror* on the cover of the March 6, 1954, issue of *Saturday Evening Post*.

she is at a moment of transition into the young adulthood that they represent. She has a lot on her mind. The discarded child's doll sits awkwardly toppled, nearly out of frame while symbols of femininity—the red lipstick and the comb and brush—lie just below her seat, suggesting proximity and immediacy. The girl's expression is caught in a moment of intense contemplation. In her lap a magazine lies open, its upturned spine echoed in the girl's furrowed brow, turned to an image of sex symbol Jane Russell, who in 1953 had erupted with scandal alongside Marilyn Monroe in the film musical *Gentlemen Prefer Blondes*. The seated girl's hair part rhymes with the magazine's centerfold, suggesting the contents of the magazine are on her mind—her thoughts about her future parting like a page turning in a book. Her clenched forearms and knees echo this wavering thin line, giving the impression so common in adolescence of feeling trapped within her own body. And sadness is something evident. Like Garland and O'Brien across from each other in the snow, this girl and her reflection are separated by something so thin yet so impenetrable. What is this sadness between them?

Meanwhile, Jane Russell's sultry face stares blankly up to the girl. Russell is in the center of the magazine on the girl's lap, but she is also in the center of the magazine readers held. That very same March 6, 1954, issue of *Saturday Evening Post* featured a "Can you name this star?" challenge with a brief bio and picture of a young girl, hair up, wearing a dark sweater. The answer was Jane Russell—here a young girl in the center of the magazine, a near-perfect inversion of Rockwell's girl in the mirror on the front cover. We realize that the glossy magazine we are holding is a mirror.

Hovering above the girl's head is the issue's headline: "The GI's Who Fell for the Reds." Inside the magazine ran a story by William A. Ulman about the failure of some American POWs held captive during the Korean War to repatriate. The article's tone was panicked. We learn that American soldiers taken prisoner were indoctrinated—"brainwashed" as Edward Hunter would coin the term in 1950—as Communist sympathizers who, upon return to the United States, may act as sleeper agents.[12] Ulman interviews Sgt. Lloyd W. Pate of Columbia, South Carolina, who was held for months in a POW camp:

> "These spoiled and pampered kids—and there were lots of them, believe me—died like lice in prison camp. No guts here"—Pate pointed to his belly—"or here"—he pointed to his head. "Too much mamma," he finished laconically.

"Take me," Pate added. "I got home and what do I find the first day I'm back? My mother had been writing—out of her own head, mind you; no commie nudging needed for her—right to the President of the United States, asking he should do something to get this war over with and me home." He angrily pounded his fist into his hand. "I had to be real stern with her—real stern. I got no love for a hatful of generals, but the way I figure is that they got to be generals because they knew their business, without a bunch of interfering women and psalm singers writing congressmen, who just pass the letters on to the Army. This Army of ours just isn't tough enough to fight this new kind of war, on account of women are always softening it up. They don't want their men to be tough. Do they want them dead?"

The problem, as Pate sees it, is that mothers and wives of prisoners were making the Army soft, prone to ideological vulnerability when faced with interrogation. Another man, Sgt. Thompson Morse, also of South Carolina, echoed this point: "A guy that's worried all the time about his guts or his girl is easy meat to a Red," adding, "The way I figure is the way the Bible says, 'There shall be hewers of wood and drawers of water.'"[13]

The real issue, as Ulman sees it, is that most soldiers entered the war with little to no idea what Communism was. When taught principles of Communism under duress in these prison camps, it was too late. Their surfaces cracked. Now the haunting question was how many of these soldiers were back at home, their broken surfaces hiding a grief below—the grief of *how to be home*, the sorrow of *knowing too much*, the sadness of *surviving*.

Ulman's story, covered in the veneer of Rockwell's furrowed girl in the mirror, arrived only nine months after Operation Big Switch had swapped prisoners of war held by American, Chinese, and Korean military prisons. Over three thousand American soldiers were returned home. Eventually all but six of them repatriated. All but six.

Almost one year to the day after the Korean Armistice Agreement was signed, Americans saw in *Seven Brides for Seven Brothers* six woodsmen frozen in fear and sadness—hewers of wood, as the POW put it. They sing about lost love, yes, but what I hear is an anxious foil for the grief looming over the entire film. Amid tremendous fatigue and displacement in America, soldiers returning from Korean prison camps were asked to flip a switch. Repatriate. Forget about it. Like the girls in the film, some of the prisoners eventually fell in love with their captors (or at least their ideology) and didn't know how to come home the same. Ever the poet of the people, Robert Frost might have spoken for many when, in a September 1954 interview with Ray Josephs, he told the country it was time to move on: "In three words, I can sum up everything I've learned about life. It goes on. In all the confusions of today, with all our troubles . . . with politicians and people slinging the word fear around, all of us become discouraged . . . tempted to say this is the end, the finish. But life—it goes on. It always has. It always will. Don't forget that."[14]

For me, the final scene meets a fine point with only one word: *justified*. All parties are justified, not happy. The film ends with a wedding, of course. Unsure whether Milly's baby might actually be the child of one of the captive women, the pious townspeople are left with no choice but to hastily marry off all the women to their captors. They feel justified. In a shotgun wedding—literally, since the girls' fathers oversee the wedding with rifles in hand—the six Pontipee brothers are married to their six captives. Brides and grooms feel justified. The final scene of seven grooms kissing their new brides while weeping fathers with rifles bear witness squeaks by as joyous only because the swelling orchestra brings back one last time the churchy strains of "Sobbin' Women." The audience feels justified. The scene freeze echoes Frost's point: life goes on, the end justifies the means.

But the end is so hasty and so flimsily managed that it's hard to know if this is really a happy ending for anyone. There is no closing song. The wedding, so common a tool of musical theater's reconciliatory aesthetic, happens here under duress and so loses its power. A forced reconciliation down the barrel of the gun echoes the kind of tidy ending Aunt Eller manages with her pistol at the close of *Oklahoma!* but in *Seven Brides for Seven Brothers* the community folds under its own villainy. *Oklahoma!* kills off Jud Fry so that the community can heal; *Seven Brides for Seven Brothers* sacrifices the community so that its version of Jud Fry, the lonely Pontipee brothers, can heal. The moral in both seems to be that violence and muscle win the day. The lesson behind the moral seems to be the grief we build and the grief that freezes us to the core. Hewers of wood, drawers of water.

There is a moment in *Seven Brides for Seven Brothers* that, for all the times I watched it growing up, I had repeatedly misheard. It happens early in the film, just after the second musical number. Adam has married Milly and, unbeknownst to her, is bringing her home to a rowdy and crowded farm with six other adult brothers—all uncouth and dirty and lonely. Once introduced to them all, a shocked Milly looks down at the small bouquet of herbs she gathered along the trek from town to holler. "I guess I should have picked some more sorrel," she says. But I always heard her say *sorrow—I should have picked some more sorrow.*

That mishearing is like a wave along the film's surface, a distorted mirror, through a glass darkly. I want to follow my mishearing of that moment into the following chapter because I believe it peeks below to see what screen musicals didn't want or didn't know how to be known: the sorrow none of us knew we brought with us on the journey.

THIRD STAGE

Bargaining

The bargaining is really an attempt to postpone; it has to include a prize offered "for good behavior," it also sets a self-imposed "deadline," and it includes an implicit promise that the patient will not ask for more if this one postponement is granted. . . . Most bargains are made with God and are usually kept a secret or mentioned between the lines or in a chaplain's private office.

—Kübler-Ross, *On Death and Dying*, 73

CHAPTER 3

Dead God

John Lennon loaded the gun that killed him when in an interview with the *Evening Standard* on March 4, 1966, he told the world that rock 'n' roll might very well outlast Christianity. "We're more popular than Jesus now," he said of the Beatles.

A radical statement to utter but surely not a secret to many. Church attendance in the UK was in steady decline, and religious leaders throughout Europe, including Pope John XXIII and his successor, Paul VI, scuttled for solutions to bring Christianity more in line with a changing, challenging world. The religious nerves among American Christians were far more exposed, however, and Lennon's statement confirmed for many the worry that rock 'n' roll was a vehicle for antireligious dark forces in the world. Fourteen years later, on December 8, 1980, Mark David Chapman gunned Lennon down on the doorstep of the Dakota apartment building in New York City. He later cited his grievance with Lennon's statement as a motivating factor for killing him.[1]

Lennon's interview arrived at a crucial moment in American political discourse. Four weeks later, *Time* magazine featured a cover that, for the first time ever, and with tremendous controversy, withheld a cover image in favor of only three words printed in red against a black background: "Is God Dead?"

An army of letters to the editor stormed the magazine, and edited collections on the subject appeared shortly thereafter. Nietzsche, with his death-of-God sentiment, was resurrected from the nineteenth century to do battle in the twentieth. Tellingly, this was read as an anti-American question rather than an expressly anti-religious one. "TIME's story is biased,

FIGURE 3.1 Cover of *Time*, April 8, 1966.

pro-atheist and pro-Communist, shocking and entirely un-American," wrote one reader.

God was a central player in so many American debates of the 1960s, including the battles against Communism at home and in far-flung places, as well as a red-hot war for civil rights long denied under presumptions of liberty that threaded religion with bigotry. Evidence mounted against God being whatever God had once been. If God wasn't already dead, *Time* and John Lennon both seemed to be saying, then the end surely was near. Christians and Christian leaders, in turn, felt that the solution was to scrub away as much daylight as possible between the world and religion. A living God is harder to deny when the good of his people is so clearly spreading into a broken world.

Only one month after Lennon's "We're more popular than Jesus now" bit, the jukebox film musical *The Singing Nun* (1966) appeared in theaters. Based on the life of Jeannine Deckers, a nun in Brussels whose folk singing skyrocketed her to international acclaim, and featuring music by Deckers and Harry Sukman, *The Singing Nun* centers on the belief that Christians ought to diminish any distance between religion and the everyday world. Sister Ann, as she is called in the musical (and portrayed by Debbie Reynolds), is caught between music and the religious order. She tries to do both but ultimately fails. In bargaining to save the life of a boy named Dominic, Sister Ann promises God to give up her musical career and devote her life fully to serving the needs of the poor. The boy lives; she is last seen in the film serving a remote village in Africa.

This chapter explores the bargain that Sister Ann strikes with God against the crisis of faith in which Americans were engulfed in the 1960s. *The Singing Nun* offers a tidy solution—you make religion and America better by making them seem less different. But the film also raises less certain questions about what happens to religion when it looks like the rest of the world and what happens to the everyday world when the sacred is no longer possible. The real Jeannine Deckers fell into a spiraling faith crisis, depression, and in-patient treatments due, at least in part, to her inability to fully leave one world for the other. In some ways, this makes Jeannine's life an intriguing encapsulation of this moment where religion and the world feel bound together. In bargaining away one thing for the other, Jeannine unknowingly delivered herself to a diminished version of both. As Saint Matthew records, "Ye cannot serve God and mammon."

Is God dead? This question marks the grief at the heart of our story.

From 1962 to 1965, the Second Vatican Council redressed the Catholic Church, shoring up the ancient institution against the swiftly changing world at midcentury. Liturgy in the vernacular was now an option. Nuns were encouraged to relax their demeanors and clothing, to be more visible in communities where they were needed most. The solutions sought were not to make the church further entrenched or set apart, however, but instead were designed to foment a renewed church order where values central to religious life spilled into and abounded in the everyday world. Church leaders spoke of a "Catholic spring" that was soon to burst forth.

In retrospect, this position sounds indistinguishable from the American brand of Christian conservatism that would rise to power in the 1970s and 1980s—a worldview that sought to close the gap between religion and the political and make America a more explicitly Christian nation once more. In practice, however, the Second Vatican represented a push not for purifying the world but rather for expanding Christian values of care, mercy, and welfare into the world.

The role of nuns was particularly rethought, both in and outside of the Church. In 1963, Cardinal Suenens of Belgium (where Jeannine Deckers lived and sang, you might recall) published an influential book, *The Nun in the World*, that sought some kind of bridge between the refuge of God's church and the world spinning farther and farther out of its orbit. This, he acknowledged, is a tremendously challenging position to hold. The Christian today "must have his own genius—that is, he needs the Spirit of the Lord to enlighten him and inspire his enthusiasm—but he must also know the spirit of his time, its susceptibilities and reactions. Since he belongs to two worlds, that of God and that of mankind, he can only be the mediator between them if he is at the same time loyal to both."[2] The biggest share of this burden fell upon the shoulders of the Church's most visible liaison between it and the world, the nun.

A guitar-clad, folk-singing nun in 1966—one year after Bob Dylan goes electric and within months of John Lennon's controversial claim that the Beatles were more famous than Jesus—seems anachronistic. But in the annals of popular culture, these times were a-changin' together. Bob Dylan

FIGURE 3.2 Cover of *Saturday Evening Post*, July 30, 1966. Bob Dylan, now harboring a new identity and purpose in America, featured alongside Michael Novak's story "The New Nuns."

graced the cover of *Saturday Evening Post* on July 30, 1966, his downcast profile (with cigarette pursed between lips a lit fuse as far as Americans were concerned) puts Dylan in company of Roman rulers etched onto coins. "Bob Dylan: Rebel king of rock 'n' roll" the cover reads. In this age new kings were alive and aplenty. Aging gods had a harder time surviving the 1960s.

If Dylan's image here spends like a denarius, then the other side of that kingly coin is hinted at just above his head. At the top of the page reads another headline, a report by journalist Michael Novak on what he called "The New Nuns." The piece explains how nuns were still performing tasks like teaching and nursing that were once severely needed; now that others have occupied those roles, nuns today are "merely useful." Their clothes and discipline were also hallmarks of a very different time. And even more difficult, Novak writes, is the lagging conflict between a young nun eagerly joining a post–Vatican II Church and those older nuns tasked with training them:

> No religious group in America can avoid facing the risks and confusions of the oncoming culture. Nor is it certain that American religion can survive the vast cultural shift it is powerless to postpone. Must religious people cling to the old comforts and the old ways? Dare they reinterpret their values and practices in new ways? Many of the Roman Catholic sisters are ready to accept that dare. They are a test case, and countless other Americans are watching them with fascination.[3]

America was indeed watching in fascination. Television in America during this time used women hiding their true identity as a comedic ploy. Sitcoms like *I Dream of Jeanie* or *Bewitched* are key examples of this narrative. The same can be said of *The Flying Nun* sitcom, which first aired one year later in 1967, and followed a nun whose small stature and enormous headwear gave her, on a windy day, the gift of flight. This strange combination of television programming suggests that young nuns present a similar problem to the communities where they are sent, appearing as the ordinary women all around them while withholding their secreted powers. Music is a part of that problem.

Novak's story mentions some young postulants arriving to the monastery with guitars in hand, clearly seeing the instrument as a valuable tool and an embodiment of the kind of future many young nuns were bargaining for. A guitar cradled in the arms of a young woman becomes something of a cultural touchpoint. This decade saw not just one but two screen musicals centering on the world and work of guitar-clad nuns. *The Singing Nun* appeared one year after the film version of Rodgers and Hammerstein's *The Sound of Music* graced theaters, and the two stories intersect in intriguing ways. Similar to Maria in *The Sound of Music*, Sister Ann carries around an acoustic guitar—at the time, clearly an emblem of

FIGURE 3.3 Top: Julie Andrews as Maria von Trapp in the 1965 film adaptation of *The Sound of Music*. Bottom: Debbie Reynolds as Sister Ann in the 1966 film *The Singing Nun*.

counterculture, but a tamer counterculture than what burgeoning rock 'n' roll symbolized. Both Maria and Sister Ann arrive in the corrupt city from an idyllic rural world, their gendered purity wrinkled by an instrument tokenizing the comfort of everyday people while also provocatively cradled intimately against the body. Images of both Sister Ann and Maria von Trapp with their guitars share focus with images of aristocratic women and their guitars as painted from the Renaissance through the end of the nineteenth century with Renoir's 1897 *The Guitar Player.*

Leonard Bernstein would use the acoustic guitar for similar, albeit less sensual, purposes across the shoulders of the Celebrant in his *Mass*, commissioned to open the Kennedy Center in 1977. The Celebrant suffers a faith crisis throughout the mass, the guitar he carries being a symbol of a much greater burden of shouldering belief in a disbelieving world. That score's opening guitar chords strum forth the lyric "Sing God a simple song," the C sharp of "God" lingering uncomfortably over the G and D sustained fifth, a hollowed-out G major chord—forming a tri-tone, the devil's interval, a marker of hard things to come. The figure of Jesus and the symbol of the guitar, for better or for worse, were by the 1960s threaded together. Bob Dylan going electric and John Lennon seriously comparing rock 'n' roll to Jesus were inflammatory gestures best understood in relation to the broader strategy that *The Singing Nun* puts forward—that is, how to use music to be both in and of the world.

In 1964 philosopher Arthur C. Danto attended an exhibition of Andy Warhol's *Brillo Box* and became convinced that the art world would never again be the same. Danto published that year his influential essay "The Artworld," where he began to formulate what would later become the central thesis of his career—that is, art had ended.

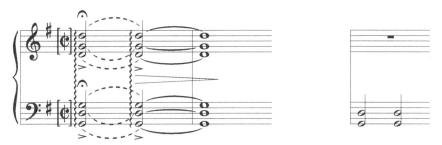

EXAMPLE 3.1 Opening chords of Leonard Bernstein's *Mass* (left) compared with the open chords of Molly Brown's left hand (right).

I fold Danto into the discussion here because the thrust of his claims pushes the controversy amid *The Singing Nun* into some broader clarity. First, Danto makes the claim that there are times when a philosophy of art—that is, a history and theory of art—is required to determine when and if something is in fact a work of art. This itself is an extension of Clement Greenberg's theories from the early 1960s, which presupposed that what we call art had been invented sometime around the sixteenth century; prior to that point, the concept of art as something set apart and essentially a commentary upon the world simply was not conceivable.[4] If art held a beginning, Danto claimed, then surely it might also have a conclusion. With great provocation, Danto supposes that art ended with Warhol in the sense that art no longer held a distinction between itself and the everyday objects in the world. No longer vying for a sacred or set-apart status, art had to justify something of itself precisely because the *Brillo Box* called art and the Brillo box in the grocery store held no reasonable differences, at least no differences beyond what could be consulted through a philosophy. Art had proven itself possible without constraint by collapsing the space held sacred between it and the world.[5]

This is a question of narratives, not art per se. Painting, sculpture, and drawing continue past Warhol unabated, of course, but the narrative guiding art's historical trajectory does not. Now we live in an age without art, which is to say an age where the conditions of something being art are absolute and without restriction. Anything can be a work of art. That's what it means for art to end.

Danto's question "Why am I a work of art?" rhymes with the question haunting religion at this time—"Why am I a religious person?" Charles Taylor attempts to unwind this warp in his book *A Secular Age*, which wonders aloud how, through the mechanism of the Enlightenment, societies evolved from a place where religion was an essential and universal explanation for the world to one now where religion is but one explanation among many on offer.[6] Taylor's work and Danto's work overlap in that they acknowledge that both religion and art were once so tightly wrapped within daily living that it might never have occurred to a person to call this or that thing, ritual, or practice *religious* or *artistic*.

Those days have passed. With Warhol we have finally reached a point where any master narrative guiding art into a relationship with the broader world had run out of fuel. Art ended. Art became philosophy. And of religion?

What seems to be happening alongside art's fulfillment of its historical arc during the 1960s is the emergence of a Christian narrative that hopes to redefine Christianity's relationship with mammon. It is not to say that Christianity or religion ended along with art. But given the fevered pitch of the *Time* magazine question "Is God Dead?" surely the calculation changed something of the equation itself. In closing the gap between the sacred and the profane, Christian communities were thrusting themselves in the same direction as the countercultural movements: diminishing hierarchies of race, gender, sexuality, and so on. What world closes under these conditions? When religion and mammon collapse into each other (or one into the other), what purpose does religion serve? Is religion absolved in a world that struggles to tell the two apart? What compromises? What gains? What losses? And most common to the worlds of art and the worlds of religion is the belief that something else—something better, something *outside*, at least—is possible. For either to end, those ideals and values about the sacred also teeter on the edge. This is where musicals come back into the picture.

In *The Singing Nun*, Sister Ann is encouraged to use her musical gifts to reach a broad audience of both believers and nonbelievers. Her skills were special, and the fact of her being a nun only made her contributions that more attractive. Throughout the musical, Sister Ann struggles to understand her competing feelings and allegiances, one to the religious work she clearly loves and another to the acclaim her music brings her. Her confused situation is made all the more strained by her producer, a man named Robert Gerarde (played by Chad Everett), who we learn, before she had entered the abbey, was her sweetheart. Their obvious attraction to each other throughout the film—and his awakening from crude and rushed music businessman to one more in touch with his emotional and musical contributions—mirrors the story of Maria and Captain von Trapp. It is Maria who coaxes music back into the home of the von Trapps, saving the children from their father and him from himself. Sister Ann does the same. Music in both stories brings nun and callous man together. In *The Sound of Music*, Maria leaves the Church for her love. In *The Singing Nun*, Sister Ann finally chooses the Church over music, and Robert is left behind.

But Robert is not the central love interest for Sister Ann. Throughout the story, Sister Ann befriends a young and motherless boy named Dominic. Her first megahit, in fact, is a song named both for him and

Saint Dominique, the namesake of her abbey in Brussels. Sister Ann's relationship with Dominic's teenage sister (and de facto mother), Nicole, is in some ways an inverted mirror. Nicole feels guilty because she often wants to leave Dominic to go out into the world and have a life of her own. Sister Ann feels guilty for how being partway in the world means she, too, is leaving (Saint) Dominique/Dominic. Dominique/Dominic lies at the center of these two women's worlds. Both women are young and we get the impression that both feel youth is setting them into trouble. It is telling that Nicole and her family move to the country at the story's end, paralleling Sister Ann's departure from the country into the "ideal" (as in, needs plenty of help) urban community. In the end, Sister Ann, too, leaves for the country—the countryside and villages of Africa.

After Sister Ann's success in music, Dominic gets hit by a car because the gate to the abbey is left open. "The gate must remain closed at all times," Sister Ann scolds a mother just moments before, and yet she herself has left the figurative gate open between the world and the cloistered abbey.

At least this is how the film ends. *The Singing Nun* coalesces around these questions with a screenplay by Sally Bowers, whose own life story gave rise to the 1944 film musical *Meet Me in St. Louis* (Bowers's alter ego, Tootie, stands in the snowy yard across from sadness then and now). This is the last screenplay Bowers completed before her death. Struggling openly with addiction, loneliness, and depression, Bowers's life tracks oddly against these two musicals: one marking the beginning of her life and the other representing the final chapter of it. In *The Singing Nun*, Bowers wraps up the story with a happy though uncertain ending. The sister has given up music but is doing the Lord's work, powered by the thrust of a vehicle named after her biggest musical success. If there is a middle ground to be struck, *The Singing Nun* somewhat desperately finds it in this rough conclusion.

After originating the role of darling Kathy Selden in *Singin' in the Rain* (1952), Debbie Reynolds flooded into a dynamic career on stage and screen. It was her role as Molly Brown in Meredith Willson's 1964 film adaptation of the musical *The Unsinkable Molly Brown* that painted Reynolds as the feisty, strong-headed girl next door. Her association with Brown was so strong that she titled her final memoir *Unsinkable*—a reference in the film to both Brown's survival on the ill-fated *Titanic* as well as her remarkable rags-to-riches ascent as a newcomer into America's fabulously wealthy upper echelons.

In *The Unsinkable Molly Brown*, Reynolds plays a convincing tomboy—a rugged mountain woman with modest yet unreachable goals for herself. She wants to learn how to read and write. She wants to have nice things in her home. And she wants to have a jug of whiskey always available for her adoptive father, Shamus. True to Willson's charming gambit with Harold Hill in *The Music Man* (which had its own film adaptation released in 1962, only two years earlier), Molly Brown sees her luck change when she is able to make a new life in a new town by faking her way through a couple of piano chords. Asleep at the piano one night, Molly's left hand falls hard against an open fifth. *Clang.* She wakes with a start, discovers the power of the sturdy yet undefined sonority, and the scene fades into her new life as an entertainer, comping a lousy hand into a winning one. Those open sonorities gave her enough consonance to pass as a pianist and enough space for her to fit into. Accompanying herself as a singing barmaid, Brown urges her clients to "belly up to the bar"—a bar that she makes room for in the same way her open chord finds room for more than one modality and in the same spirit that she hopes folks make room for her.

FIGURE 3.4 Molly Brown discovers the open fifth—two points on a map of belonging.

EXAMPLE 3.2 The open chords pry open and then
hold steady, space for a new life.

The Unsinkable Molly Brown, like *The Music Man*, feels nostalgic, big-hearted, and sentimental. We cheer for Molly and her husband, Johnny, as they struggle to find acceptance amid the snobbish old money of Denver's high society. Brown is perhaps a better American icon than Harold Hill—an unsteady character who, after all, is playing a long con—but her story also feels more haunted by the America of its time.[7] Brown's insistence that all belong, and Willson's insistence that all you need is a couple of chord changes to make a life possible, overlap strangely with the civil rights demonstrations happening underfoot. This singing barmaid preached acceptance at the lunch counter while lunch counter sit-ins and protests made towns and cities from Greensboro to Oklahoma City go belly up throughout the late 1950s and early 1960s. President Lyndon B. Johnson signed into law the Civil Rights Act of 1964 only three weeks after *The Unsinkable Molly Brown* premiered in theaters. Her grit and come-from-nothing flair, her confidence and brazen belief in a better world ahead, all make Molly Brown an emblem of inclusion if not radical acceptance. Belly up to the bar, she belts. Belly up, indeed.

Two years later in *The Singing Nun*, Debbie Reynolds paints a much different picture. Solemn and studied, her Sister Ann feels disconnected from the world, a figure of exclusion. And yet her relationships with matters of race feel like they pick up where Molly Brown left them. When Sister Ann first arrives to her new post in the city, she befriends Sister Mary, a Black nun from Africa. Sister Ann and Sister Mary share a love of music and of Africa, though Sister Ann has only ever dreamed of visiting and learning the culture. Fitting for a musical, Sister Ann is most interested in the music of African devotion. Sister Mary, played by Juanita Moore (best known for her portrayal as Annie Johnson in the 1959 race relations film

Imitation of Life), tells Sister Ann that the African choirs are something to behold.

In the final frames of the movie, we see Sister Ann and Sister Mary inoculating young children in an outdoor health clinic somewhere in Africa. The scene is intended to signal Sister Ann's fulfillment in accepting the bargain she has made with God. The final music overlaid during these moments is not from Deckers's discography, which also punctuates Sister Ann's turn away from music and toward the world God calls her to serve. Instead, audiences hear the Kyrie from *Missa Luba*, a Congolese version of the Latin mass composed by Belgian priest Father Guido Haazen and recorded in 1958 by Les Troubadours du Roi Baudouin. The Congo was a Belgian colony until 1960 when it gained independence, followed immediately by the Congo Crisis (1960–1965), yet another proxy conflict between the Soviet Union and the United States.

EXAMPLE 3.3 The oscillating G minor and F major chords in the Kyrie from *Missa Luba* (1958).

Which is fitting since this selection sounds in conflict. Oscillating repeatedly between G minor and F major chords, the Kyrie—*Lord, have mercy*—is set in the style of a *kasala*, a song of mourning. On the one hand, the simplicity of the tune echoes the open fifth chords Molly Brown realizes while asleep at the piano, moralizing the accessibility and immediacy of music as a measurement of belonging and acceptance. On the other hand, the piece feels contentedly unsettled. Refusing to resolve or evolve, the Kyrie, like Sister Ann, is caught in an in-between. It is a fitting soundtrack for this singing nun who, as we will see, struggled to find solid footing in an era consumed by elements of authenticity. The recording by Les Troubadours du Roi Baudouin has since been sampled and repurposed broadly, a compelling and early example of a burgeoning "world music" genre—a genre that itself would become another pawn in the proxy war of pop music genres vying for claims of authenticity.

And authenticity feels like a summation of this entire musical, this entire moment in history, to be frank. It is not coincidental that both *The Sound of Music* and *The Singing Nun* feature folk-singing religious workers. By the mid-1960s, folk music was a tolerable gesture toward hipness, realness, authenticity. The American folk revival had reached its full-throated peak by 1965, weakened by the British invasion of bands like the Beatles and folk hero Bob Dylan's move toward recording with rock 'n' roll rhythm sections and performing with an electric guitar at the Newport Folk Festival. Folk had once been the edgy vehicle delivering hard-hitting American truths; now rock 'n' roll held the burden of authority and subversion in a world burning through saviors like kindling. More popular than Jesus and all that.

Clearly this tussle between whatever folk once represented and whatever values rock 'n' roll threatened to bring into America were being worked out in *The Singing Nun*. Sister Ann is anachronistic, relevant only in the eyes of a fading generation. We see early in the film a brush between Sister Ann and a ridiculous-looking band of four men calling themselves the Mexican Marauders, whose dress and posture bait them not only as inauthentic rocksters but, as the cover of August 27, 1966, *Saturday Evening Post* shows, as reflections of the Beatles themselves. Nonetheless, we see throughout the film that young people like this music, enjoy dancing to it, and often are doing so under the influence of alcohol or drugs. Folk and rock are set far apart in this film, proxies in a war of good and evil, perhaps, though also statements about the past and the future.

FIGURE 3.5 Cover of *Saturday Evening Post*, August 27, 1966. Compare the dress here of the Beatles (top) with the Mexican Marauders in *The Singing Nun* (bottom).

Phyllis Johnson was on vacation in Aspen, Colorado, when she hit on a new concept. The former editor of *Women's Wear Daily* and *Advertising Age*, Johnson felt constricted by the traditional format of a magazine. She had the idea for a multimedia magazine that could highlight the full possibility of modern culture, a culture she felt was idyllically captured by the artsy environment of Aspen, Colorado. In 1965 *Aspen: The Magazine in a Box* was born.

Each issue was an actual box. The box might hold phonographs, letters, printed and bound essays, along with swatches of materials and samples from advertisers. It was unique and vanguard, so it attracted and featured commentary from the likes of John Cage, Marshall McLuhan, Susan Sontag, and Andy Warhol. At the same time, it was quite cumbersome and therefore the magazine was short-lived. The final issue was mailed out in 1971.

Tucked inside the 1967 double issue of *Aspen* was a short, grouchy essay by French literary critic Roland Barthes provocatively titled "The Death of the Author." By this time, Barthes was an established thought leader of postmodernist literary theory, and the fact that this essay appeared in English *before* French speaks to his rising stock among artists and philosopher types in America. Barthes's essay is uncharacteristically short and clear. Readers should no longer feel constrained in their interpretations of literary works by the biography or intentions of the author, he argues, claiming that "a text's unity lies not in its origins but in its destination."[8] *Author*, so long etymologically tethered to our concept of *authority* or *authenticity*, was a term that ought to be dismantled, killed off, perhaps, so that the reader might finally be born.

"The Death of the Author" rattled around in the same *Aspen* box as a score and recording of a 1964 percussion piece by Morton Feldman titled "The King of Denmark." Feldman's piece is an example of graphic notation. The performer is given nearly full rein in determining pitches, contour, and other musical decisions that the technology of Western notation had evolved to grant solely to the composer. Feldman, like his mentor and friend John Cage (whose work *Fontana Mix-Feed, Nov. 6, 1967* was also included in this issue), had been speaking much the same language as Barthes's essay. Cage's indeterminate compositional style had the effect of disturbing the encrusted and distinct categories of performer, composer, and audience and instead encouraged all three to be present at once. Eliminating or diminishing the control and influence of the author was essential to liberating musical meaning into the world.

Barthes's dead author pinged like a ricochet off the previous year's *Time* magazine issue concerning a dead god. Both impulses are for a reordered world: an egalitarian approach to everything from reading a text to following your bliss. With dead authors and dead gods, authority might then finally be redistributed like a tax credit back to the living masses.

With this newfound authority burning a hole in their pockets, Americans quickly invested this authority a number of ways but perhaps most prominently in the aura of the popular artist. Susan Sontag's essay "The Aesthetics of Silence," which appeared alongside Barthes's "The Death of the Author," is keen on this problem, noting that the empty spirituality of the age was being cast fairly or unfairly upon art—such a thing too exhausted and burdened from the nineteenth century to withstand that level of belief and empowerment in what was becoming a postmodern age. Silence, then, became an aesthetic of supreme value. Not saying or speaking anything. Becoming, in an era of a disappeared and muted God, uncannily god-like in choosing silence over presence. Dead God, dead authors, dead artists. What, we must ask, was *not* stretching into a coffin?

This conundrum pulls back the curtain on *The Singing Nun*'s division between folk, rock 'n' roll, and ultimately world music as emblems of authority. Sister Ann emerges into a world using the tools of a has-been god (folk music) that bears too close a resemblance to, and proves no match for, the Baal of youth culture (rock 'n' roll). The final scene's surrender to the *Missa Luba* ought to be a return to the Catholic values of spirituality and universality. But instead the piece feels like a solution to a parallel war over authority and authenticity. World music, universal and possible and sharing no hereditary likeness to the previous gods, is the horse this film finally backs. Not quite folk, not quite rock 'n' roll, not quite old, but also not really new. It's the best solution in a world littered with dead gods and silent artists. Let the people speak.

In pulling tight the seams connecting the everyday and the sacred, religious communities in the 1960s risked forfeiting something essential. Of course, the world felt itself unraveling in ways nuns playing guitars could hardly account for. Arthur C. Danto's observations about the master narrative of art ("there is an era of imitation, followed by an era of ideology, followed by our post-historical era in which, with qualification, anything goes") feels oddly prescient.[9] *Anything goes* cuts both ways. An invitation to understand the power of God in new, fresh ways. More refined vocabulary to name the loneliness of a world populated with gods in competition with gods. How did art, which was ending, attend to these dynamic changes among religious communities?

In his book *Saving Abstraction*, musicologist Ryan Dohoney accounts for the rise in religious (specifically Catholic) interest in abstract art during the 1960s. Dramatically and unexpectedly, abstract expressionism saw a tremendous upswing of interest in the 1960s, eclipsing realist artists like Edward Hopper or Norman Rockwell so quickly that the artists banded together to fight what they deemed to be panic buying of works by Mark Rothko and Philip Guston by the Museum of Modern Art. Dohoney's book attends specifically to the oil magnates John and Dominique de Menils, who in 1965 envisioned and commissioned Mark Rothko to complete the Rothko Chapel in Houston, Texas (opened in 1971) and the musical work *Rothko Chapel* by Morton Feldman.[10] Catholic patrons began seeing abstract art as a mechanism of the divine—a style that resisted a strained and tired vocabulary for God, allowing simultaneously maximum flexibility and fidelity to belief systems. Abstraction proved to offer a valuable aloofness and a prized enchantment to whomever most needed it whenever they most needed it. Rothko died before the chapel was opened, but the site continues to serve as one of the most prominent contributions to ecumenical art in the twentieth century.

But it was not Mark Rothko and his enormous canvases of thickly painted rectangles but rather Andy Warhol and his Brillo boxes and soup cans that seemed to capture the everyday energy of the moment. Pop art was to abstract expressionism as rock 'n' roll was to the folk movement—subversions of the subversive. Feverishly antielite and antiestablishment, the pop art movement sampled the ubiquitous marketing slogans and clouded judgment about where the everyday and the transfigured meet. Postmodernism, fueled by the remnant exhaust of puttering master narratives, was clenching its fist tighter. Rothko can fare no better than Hopper or Rockwell without a narrative. Anything can go when anything goes.

Into this arena stepped Corita Kent, or Sister Corita as she was known at the time. A forward-thinking "new nun" as Michael Novak might have called her, Sister Corita headed the Department of Art and Design at Immaculate Heart College in Los Angeles, California. Inspired by the pop art movement and its bold absorption of the busy, noisy, crowded urban everyday, Sister Corita learned how to silkscreen and began producing religious pop art with tremendous success. Theologian Harvey Cox saw in her an "*urban* sensibility," a sensibility uniquely befitting these new nuns of the world. "Like a priest, a shaman, a magician, she could pass her hands over the commonest of the everyday, the superficial, the oh-so-ordinary, and make it a vehicle of the luminous, the only, and the hope-filled," he later wrote.[11]

Sister Corita's art samples slogans and printed words from everywhere and anywhere, reconfiguring the commonplace into a mystical and religious sacred. "If we separate ourselves from the great arts of our time," she wrote, "we cannot be leaven enriching our society from within. We may well be peripheral to our society—unaware of its pains and joys, unable to communicate with it, to benefit from it or to help it."[12] As if on cue, her artwork titled *that they may have life* from 1964 borrows from the Wonder Bread polka-dot packaging and speaks to religion as the leavening agent in the world, the ingredient that gives rise and shape and possibility though no taste.

But this message is hardly full-throated. Sister Corita succeeds, and in many ways models success, as a new nun by tying together the tails of both the sacred and the profane. Her work is a visual corollary to the music Sister Ann produced during this same era. But in 1967 Sister Corita left her religious order. The real singing nun, Jeannine Deckers, left soon after. It became impossible for these women to continue living a life as a new nun, straddled between worlds designed to be incompatible. It's not likely that an absent God drove them out, but it is possible that a society determined to put women in the middle of competing absences subtracted something from both.

Jeannine Deckers, *The Singing Nun*'s Sister Ann, did not enjoy the happy ending the musical imposes on her story. Deckers left the religious order and, in so leaving, forfeited not only her name but the rights to her music connected to that name. She fought legal battles continually over the years, then attempted to move *back* into the auspices of the religious order and failed at every turn. "If we are no longer rewarded in heaven for our suffering," Elisabeth Kübler-Ross explains, "then suffering becomes purposeless in itself."[13] On March 29, 1985, at the age of fifty-one, Jeannine Deckers, the actual singing nun, took her own life.

He may not have had Maria von Trapp in mind, and certainly wasn't considering the new film musical *The Singing Nun*, but Michael Novak ended his piece on "The New Nuns" like the curtain call of a musical, on a note of optimism:

> As the new sisters set about creating a new style of religious life, they become the vanguard of all Americans who believe in God and who trust

that "the glory of God is man fully alive." The sisters come from farther back than most other groups; their rules and traditions date from long ago. But if they can maintain their integrity, their love, their passion for justice, in the world of computers, supermarkets and slums, there is hope for all of us.[14]

It was a changing technological world that Novak feels most in awe of here, a strikingly different world from the kind nuns first entered into in this country. The burden is not living this life but living somehow a life spread across competing value systems. Nuns wore a public face challenging women's autonomy and agency while at the same time under the firm guidance of a patriarchal and exclusionary worldview. How far could nuns really go in their effort to be *in* but not *of* the world? It's a marketable idea. It's an idea born from grieving a passing world. It's a citation of a world that really cannot be possible. Anything goes.

It also feels like a bargaining chip with or against God, the kind of card game Anne Sexton plays with God when finally, at the conclusion of her poetry collection *The Awful Rowing toward God*, she reaches the place where God dwells. She plays a royal flush. God plays five aces, having called a wild card when she wasn't paying attention. They both laugh and laugh and laugh at the absurdity of it all, the kindness of it all, the relief of it all. "Dearest dealer," the poem concludes, "I with my royal straight flush, / love you so for your wild card, / that untamable, eternal, gut-driven *ha-ha* / and lucky love."[15]

Bargaining is the part of the grief process that feels most elusive to Kübler-Ross. It is a knowing stage, evidence the grief has grown a bit older. Our terms are often so modest—one more day, one more hour, one more year and I'll give anything—that a winning hand hardly seems the point. It is also a stage that pivots hardest toward reality. It says, I know things will soon change and I want to pump the brakes a little. I am willing to live in that uncertain in-between if it means I can still hold on to something of the old world. It is a transition, a secret pact with the Dearest Dealer who holds a winning hand but keeps his gaze steady. So steady, in fact, that he might just seem dead.

FOURTH STAGE

Depression

In the preparatory grief there is no or little need for words. It is much more a feeling that can be mutually expressed and is often done better with a touch of a hand, a stroking of the hair, or just a silent sitting together. . . . It is a time when too much interference from visitors who try to cheer him up hinders his emotional preparation rather than enhances it.

—Kübler-Ross, *On Death and Dying*, 77

CHAPTER 4

Good Grief

On August 6, 1945, Paul Warfield Tibbets Jr., piloting a specially made U.S. Air Force bomber he named after his mother, Enola Gay, dropped a nuclear bomb on the Japanese city of Hiroshima. Three days later, a second nuclear bomb was dropped on Nagasaki. And on August 29, exactly two weeks after Japan surrendered to the Allies, *State Fair*, Richard Rodgers and Oscar Hammerstein's only musical written directly for film, was released in theaters.

There's a rhyme hiding in these facts. *State Fair* tells the story of one farm family's eventful visit to the Iowa State Fair. When Paul Tibbets was a child, one late summer several years before her namesake plane dropped the so-named "Little Boy" on Hiroshima, Enola Gay bought her own little boy a toy airplane for one dollar. Mother and son were visiting a local fair. They lived in Iowa. We live in a poem.

Which is perhaps a pithy way of acknowledging that cultural artifacts enter into our imagination utterly burdened by the world as it is. The song-and-dance version of America's heartland that *State Fair* puts forward is, I think, at heart actually a story of missed connections, of unutterable fears, of evidence that the world had endured more but grown less. My aim in this chapter is to suture some of these connections in order to allow *State Fair* to say what since 1945 it might not have known it was saying. *Enola Gay* and *State Fair*, both vehicles into other worlds, are in my mind twisted together in sorrowful strands of *look*—by the time people saw them, it was too late.

State Fair has a peculiar provenance. It is in so many ways a strange musical. Very little has been written about it. And yet it lies in the middle of two monumental works of Rodgers and Hammerstein: the Broadway productions of *Oklahoma!* in 1943 and *Carousel* in 1945. What kind of a story can a widely available yet largely ignored musical written by the titans of American musical theater history tell, if not something about its journey into obscurity? Discovering this hiddenness is more or less what I'm setting out to do.

To tell this story, I take August 1945 as a point of departure, using *State Fair*'s premiere to cast glances backward to the 1932 novel it is based upon and its subsequent 1933 film adaptation starring Will Rogers and Janet Gaynor as well as the 1962 remake starring Pat Boone and Ann-Margret. In glancing through *State Fair*'s various incarnations, I hope you'll join with me in approaching the musical as we might approach a jigsaw puzzle. Dump the box on the table, flip the pieces right side up, and build the picture from the edges in. I think the meandering path we take putting the pieces together is the real story here. The picture we put together in the end shows a conspiracy in the most literal sense—that American grief is something we *conspire*, that is, that we *breathe together*.

Our story begins where it first ended, as the Frake family makes the long drive back home from the fair. Abel Frake muses on his family's experiences: his prize hog, Blue Boy, swept the competition; his wife, Melissa, was awarded a special plaque for her mincemeat; and his daughter, Margy, and son, Wayne, had both found love. None of the Frakes seems to be able to fully articulate this feeling, but for all their successes at the fair, the car ride home is engulfed with sadness. Abel reflects in the quiet how the family was circling back to a reality that felt as much imagined as the one they had constructed for themselves at the fair. "The Frakes had stepped for a moment into a fantasy" is how Philip Stong puts it in the 1932 novel. "Now, unchanged, they were returning to that five hundred acres where only birth and death—not even marriage—had been the only changes for four generations."[1]

State fairs exist out of time; the Frakes's car seems still caught within the fair's gravitational pull. Sites of both nostalgia and technological advancement, fairs seem to meet America's mythologies head-on. And no state fair holds quite as much poetry in America as the Iowa State Fair. As Chris

Rasmussen puts it in his book *Carnival in the Countryside*, "New Jersey has the Shore. Kentucky has the Derby. Iowa has the Fair."[2] Fairs may call to mind thrill rides and cotton candy booths today, but these gatherings brought together rural and urban populations to celebrate and learn about new advancements in agriculture and livestock management. *Look at us!* our state fairs boast again and again. Would you just *look at us.*

Pageantry and carnival give state fairs that aura of out-of-time. "Like Thanksgiving and Christmas and the Fourth of July," write Greta Pratt and Karal Ann Marling, "the fair is a fixed point on the turning wheel of time that rolls along the darkened highways of the Mississippi Valley and out onto the slumbering plains of the American heartland."[3] This timelessness of the state fair matches well with the stubborn American myth of its middle spaces as, for better or for worse, trapped in time. American musical theater seems particularly attracted to this mythology. Musicals about the middle—and about Iowa in particular—are among the most iconic in the repertoire. Meredith Willson's *The Music Man* and Rodgers and Hammerstein's *State Fair* both orbit around this idea of the prairie as some kind of Brigadoon, preserving and protecting something key to what America means, used to mean, or might someday mean. If there is possibility in America, its musicals seem to think it lies somewhere in the middle.

But in our story there is something darker brewing in the heart of America. Whatever timelessness the state fair brings to mind can be something sad just as easily as it might be something to laugh off. "I been reading a thing in a magazine," says Wayne Frake, "that proves that time is just a kind of space. You can see up and down and to both sides and in front and behind. This fellow thinks that if we were made different we could see tomorrow and yesterday just the same way—but we don't because we can only see three dimensions. But really, time is just a way of saying a direction we don't know."[4] Wayne imagines time moving like a wheel, no ending in sight.

The Frake family loops into this circularity of the fair as emblems of a forgotten time. Like his biblical namesake, Abel Frake's contributions to the gods of the day are in livestock. The gods are satisfied with his sacrifice, as long as it appears in fact to be a sacrifice. The Abels of the world are fated to be a sacrifice, to be upheld as an ideal of envy and an idol of the envious. In *State Fair*, however, we have a chance to see what happens when the scapegoat survives and lives to see his own successes. It's difficult to say that Abel's fate here is any improvement.

For her part, Melissa busily worries about boastful gains in her cooking. She eventually takes home a special plaque for her mincemeat (the secret ingredient is a huge dose of brandy, which hilariously disorients the judges) after winning blue ribbons in several categories over the years. While the rest of the family flits around the fairgrounds, Melissa mostly stays at the campsite to cook food that her family hastily rushes past and to give advice that her children kindly ignore. We get the impression that her work is important to her but taken for granted by her family. And like the "honeybee" that her name etymologically conjures, Melissa cultivates a home that increasingly feels less nuclear and more transient in a modern age. She is, after all, a specialist in preservation—pickles and mincemeat can last for years and years if prepared just right. For this reason, Melissa is perhaps more attuned to the possibility that whatever awaits them at the state fair could be trouble. When a cup breaks as she is packing their food, she takes this as an omen. "I wouldn't have cared if it had broken in camp, at State Fair time," she tells Margy. "I *planned* for it to get broken then. Something always gets broken then and I thought this would be it."

Abel and Melissa Frake have both reached the top of their line. They are affirmed by the state fair, their successes evidence that they are anything but backward. But also, the state fair continues to emphasize a nostalgic past. The Frakes continue to win, but they continue to win by playing the game assigned them by the urban folk: being rustic, keeping to tradition, remaining a foil for America's progress narrative. Look at us!

Their children, on the other hand, seem in on the game. Neither of them is a simpleton. When we meet Margy, she is "restless beyond endurance."[5] She loves something about farm life; so much of her struggle is in trying to bridge lifestyles of her urban fling with those of the life she feels devoted to. It's not exactly that the Frakes are living on the other side of modernity. Margy's beau at home is a farmer who drives a Vespa scooter and, more than any other character, is devoted to a rational, scientific scheme to improve farming efficiency. It's unclear, then, what Margy is hoping to find at the state fair, other than perhaps an affirmation that the life she leads is in fact the life she will ultimately choose rather than inherit. And isn't that the ultimate expression of American modernity, the belief that we are in fact choosing what has most likely been chosen for us?

The uncertain future of a young woman hewn from America's fertile heartland held strong allure in the popular imagination of the midcentury. Aaron Copland's 1952 opera *The Tender Land*, which was intended but failed to premiere on the small screen with the NBC Television Opera Workshop, encircles the fate of a rural way of life as young Laurie Moss contemplates ways to escape her farm community. "Time has grown so short / The world so wide," she sings with a grin at her high school graduation. Laurie does leave, is determined from the start to leave, though it is unclear at the opera's conclusion how either she or the community she leaves behind will survive without one another. Three years later, with the rollout of the film adaptation of *Oklahoma!* audiences watched another girl named Laurey secure a future on the frontier farm in large part due to the scariness and uncertainty of what lies beyond it—Kansas City, for one, as a symbol of urban modernity—but also a more complex set of questions about gender and agency and power than she is able or willing to ask.

The 1962 remake of *State Fair* introduces Margy and her sadness as another notch on the belt of this agrarian archetype. We first meet Margy as she roams the farmland, the smallness of Margy and the immensity of the land a clear nod to Andrew Wyeth's *Christina's World* from 1948. But Margy does not want to leave this way of life. She is simply unsure how to live when she seems to have everything she ever wanted. Wyeth's figure crawls amid her future. Margy stands to face it. She is brave but sad. There is a reckoning for Margy that seems to be a lasting preoccupation of America at this time: What do women in the middle really need or want from life?

Like his sister, Wayne is caught in the middle of what seem like competing worlds. But on closer inspection, the Frakes lead very modern lives. Going to the state fair is an annual family adventure that increasingly feels empty and its attractions only so-so. This is no romanticization of the rural America of yesteryear. It's a reckoning, a signal of the end of something. If natural man and urban man no longer feel estranged, then there is in fact no escape. No wizard behind the curtain. No Cain to slay Abel. "We have never been modern," Bruno Latour reminds us. This is a philosophical story, one cut from tragedy more than comedy. In the 1945 version, Melissa Frake sums this up tidily after winning the special plaque for her mincemeat: "I've got the most a woman can get in life, Margy. If I think any more about it, I'll cry."[6]

FIGURE 4.1
Margy surveying
the farm in *State
Fair* (top) evokes
the wonder and
constraint of
Andrew Wyeth's
1948 painting
Christina's World
(bottom).

What the Frakes all hold together is a melancholic question: Are we ever satisfied? *State Fair* challenges the well-worn image of prideful, humble rural families whose devotion to land and discipline are their own rewards. The Frakes are unsettled. They have everything they want and yet want something more. The grief of having everything you could ever need or want feels like the unnamed grief slouching the shoulders of so many Americans today. If you think more about it, you might cry too.

In the original film musical, Wayne is on a mission. The previous year, he had spent all his fair money at a hoop toss only to win a handsome white-handled revolver that, upon closer inspection, was just a solid piece of wood. Humiliated, Wayne has practiced all year in the barn with his mother's embroidery hoops in order to win back his losses and show the rest of the fairgoers how the games were rigged, their prizes not what they seemed. His practice pays off. Straightaway, Wayne finds the hoop toss booth and proceeds to win every time. He is so successful that the man

FIGURE 4.2 Top: Dick Haymes as Wayne Frake in the 1945 film *State Fair*, practicing the hoop toss in the barn. Bottom: Pat Boone as Wayne Frake in the 1962 film *State Fair*, gripping the steering wheel during a race.

running the booth pays him to not come back, and in Stong's original story he offers a philosophical retort to Wayne's accusations of cheap prizes: "As long as nobody wins those prizes they're just as good as they look to be." "He's selling dreams, intangibles," Stong later adds, "never meant to be scrutinized in the cold light of day."[7]

In the 1962 remake, the hoop toss scheme is dropped and instead Wayne is obsessed with a different game of circles: racing. No doubt an effort to capture the youthful energy and sex appeal of star Pat Boone, Wayne's red sports car is an upgraded symbol of his circuitous worldview. We meet Wayne in all forms of this story literally going in circles. When his new love interest, Emily (played by Ann-Margret), later asks how he knew he wanted to become a farmer, he gives away the game. "I don't think you decide," he replies. "One day you're a little boy out feeding chickens. Next thing you know you're an old man out feeding chickens. That's how you know."[8] Life runs in circles. Wayne seems preoccupied by them, gripping them tightly to win whatever game is afoot.

The 1962 remake of *State Fair* also upgrades the fair itself, moving the story from Des Moines, Iowa, to Dallas, Texas. By 1960 the population of Dallas was soaring. It was the fourteenth-largest city in America and quickly on the rise. The original setting of Iowa reinforced the nostalgic, romanticized ideal of rural America. Placing the Frakes in Texas makes their proximity to and encounter with urban sprawl much more dynamic and something of a compositional problem—Richard Rodgers swapped out the iconic tongue-twister "All I Owe Ioway" from the 1945 film with a late duet between Abel and Melissa called "The Little Things in Texas."

Moving the Frakes to Texas also put them at the heart of America's space race, an extension of whatever energy Paul Tibbets had released in 1945 with his *Enola Gay*. With the opening of the Johnson Space Center in 1961, Houston had become NASA's (and by extension, the U.S. government's) central nervous system. Texas was on everyone's minds in the spring of 1962 when astronaut John Glenn (who trained to be a pilot in Iowa) became the first man to circle the Earth in a spacecraft. Wayne driving in circles, gripping hard the wheel of his sports car, may seem far below the interests of spaceships and fears of Soviet nuclear power, but there is reason to believe Americans were looped into these sentiments. On March 9, 1962—the day *State Fair* was released in theaters—*Time* magazine featured an advertisement for fluorescent grow lamps that shortened the perceived distance between rural life and the ultramodern. A man in

FIGURE 4.3 Advertisement for fluorescent grow lamps in the March 9, 1962, issue of *Time*—the same day as the *State Fair* theatrical release.

a spacesuit waters plants, the headline reading "New fluorescent lamps grow food on spaceship 'farms.'" This just weeks before President Kennedy would open the Seattle World's Fair and give America its futuristic Space Needle—piercing the sky above like a plow breaking the prairie soil. Whatever frontier life *State Fair* originally envisioned about Iowa, by 1962 that frontier and its farmers were decidedly elsewhere, far above, making lazy circles in the sky.

Yet for all the hubbub about Texas, Wayne's climactic race scene was actually filmed at the Oklahoma State Fairgrounds, just seven miles from Oklahoma City's airport, named after Will Rogers, the original Abel Frake. Eight miles in the other direction lies Wiley Post Airport, named after the pilot adventurer who died along with Will Rogers in a fiery plane crash in 1935—three years after *State Fair* the book, two years after *State Fair* the movie, ten years before *State Fair* the film musical, and twenty-seven years before Pat Boone would circle the tracks as Wayne Frake in the second *State Fair* film musical. This scene's location is thick—a fixed point on the wheel of time—since circling a race track is equal parts chasing a dream and running from it. A loop is still a loop, no matter how fast you take the bend.

But, of course, viewers are meant to believe that the story is developing in Dallas the entire time. The Frake family sings the show's title song as they drive their 1961 Dodge Dart Phoenix convertible from their farm to the fair, changing the lyrics from "it's dollars to doughnuts" to "it's *Dallas* to doughnuts / that our state fair / is the best state fair in our state." This farm family's cheery drive into the city anticipates what viewers would see six months later with the premiere of *The Beverly Hillbillies*. The Clampetts drive a beat-up jalopy piled high with furniture and family, a clear token of poor white refugees hailing back to the Joad family fleeing Oklahoma for California in John Ford's 1940 film adaptation of *The Grapes of Wrath*. Both the Frakes and the Clampetts drive an open-air vehicle, and both carry what seems like a lifetime of hopes and dreams, but the two depictions of rural life in 1962 couldn't be further apart. The Clampetts are ignorant and silly, clear setups for laugh tracks every time they meet modern technologies. The Frakes, on the other hand, are refined, intelligent, wholesome, and are no strangers to the trappings and hauntings of urban life. Abel approaches farm and livestock with the skill of a scientist. Wayne drives a sports car on farm roads, and we meet Margy's beau, Harry, driving a Vespa scooter along the farm's fence rows. This is a family on the move, which is, I think, part of the lesson here.

The 1962 adaptation of *State Fair* wizens the Frakes and makes their encounter with the urban world less an existential conflict than an extension of their natural habits developed in the country. They are no longer the rural backwater (Frake sounds like "freak," after all) but Americans through and through. This is not to say that there isn't intergenerational conflict and a sense of caution about the changing world. Melissa cooks and sets a table for a family that never seems to gather around, while Abel mutters under his breath as Wayne speeds past in his sports car, "Twenty-two years of love and care and what do we raise? A piston farmer."[9] But on the whole, the remake diminishes the story's conflict as between urban and rural life. What gets elevated in the process, then, is the sadness that lies beneath it all.

Driving is an apt metaphor in this remake—if the *Enola Gay* haunted the 1945 musical, in 1962 it's the open road that threatens to reshape the world. By 1962 America's interstate system had connected Americans in ways unimaginable in 1945. Rural and urban life were separated by

FIGURE 4.4 Top: The Frake family drives into Dallas in their convertible in the 1962 remake of *State Fair*. Center: The Clampetts drive into Los Angeles in their jalopy in the 1962 series *The Beverly Hillbillies*. Bottom: The Kennedy motorcade driving into Dallas, November 22, 1963.

smaller and smaller increments of time. The hardships of overnight travel from farm to state fair evident in Philip Stong's original story had become normalized by the 1960s, even, as with Jack Kerouac's 1957 novel, *On the Road*, folded into the American mythos of open vistas and adventurous frontiers. Of course, roads run two ways. The Frakes could easily get to the city, but, perhaps even more significantly, whatever the city represented could just as easily get to them.

Americans witnessed this in real time. On November 22, 1963, one year after Americans saw the Frake family cheerfully singing while driving into Dallas, they now saw images of President John F. Kennedy being shot and killed while driving into Dallas. The presidential motorcade, a refitted 1961 Lincoln Continental convertible, draws a poetic scribble between Kennedy and Lincoln, as does the fact that John Wilkes Booth chose a theater as his site for murder and Lee Harvey Oswald was apprehended outside of one. But another poetic line is worth mentioning, for the Frake family's convertible drives them toward hope and possibility in Dallas just as America one year later saw the Kennedy convertible speed away from Dallas with so much of its hopes and possibilities dealt a fatal blow. Both families are caught in the open air—the air we can't help but *conspire*, breathe together. It well may be that the true conspiracy with Kennedy's murder comes clear by glancing at a film musical from one year earlier: whatever happens with this story about the Frakes, it happens to all of us.

Wayne meets Emily at the fair. Her worldly charm immediately carries Wayne away. He has a girlfriend named Eleanor waiting for him back home, but she is conventional to a tee and a poor match for Wayne. In the 1933 film and the 1945 film musical, Emily is an entertainer, either an acrobat or a lounge singer. She is wise and experienced with men and initially sees Wayne as a handsome bit of fun with whom to pass the time away. But in the 1962 remake, Ann-Margret and Pat Boone push the characters of Emily and Wayne closer to the original story, where both are sexually active and pursue each other intensely, if not with differing ideas of where exactly this relationship will go after the fair is over. *State Fair* was Ann-Margret's screen debut, starting a string of film musical appearances throughout the 1960s, including *Bye Bye Birdie* in 1963 and, most famously, starring alongside Elvis Presley—like Wayne, another race car driver but, unlike Pat Boone, a bad boy—in 1964 with *Viva Las Vegas*. Her rising star power, along with Pat Boone's wholesome appeal among both teenagers and their parents, helped correct what had been some imbalances in the 1945 version, particularly with regard to the musical numbers. In the original, Wayne falls for Emily as she sings the song "That's for Me" with her dance band. The number is diegetic—background music performed as such rather than embodied in the universe of Wayne and Emily—so it fails to carry the characters forward in any meaningful way. The show's big ensemble numbers, "It's a Grand Night for Singing" and "All I Owe Ioway," are likewise performed at a bandstand. A musical typically works by creating an alternate reality where characters sing but are largely unaware of it. Emily's compliment about Wayne's singing voice after he takes a verse again ruptures the musical's otherworldliness, further reinforcing that what happens at the fair *is the alternate reality* for these musical characters, similar to what theater audiences accept when watching characters on stage burst into song. Tellingly, the only song in *State Fair* that exists within a musical universe is Margy's "It Might as Well Be Spring," which I'll get to shortly.

In the remake, "That's for Me" is given to Wayne, who sings it to himself after meeting Emily at the racetrack, helping cement his seriousness about pursuing Emily, or at least what she represents. In turn, Emily takes Wayne's song "Isn't It Kind of Fun?" and turns it into a huge production number at the fair. Later in her hotel room, the couple sing a new addition to the show, "Willing and Eager." With Boone shirtless and Ann-Margret in a negligee, the tune's closely rubbing half steps on the words "willing"

EXAMPLE 4.1 "Willing and Eager." Music and lyrics by Richard Rodgers.

and "eager" pull Wayne and Emily closer, musically simulating the con-
summation of their relationship.

Another addition to the remake is a song for Margy's new love interest,
Jerry (Pat in the original, and played by Bobby Darin in the remake), called
"This Isn't Heaven." Jerry's crooning and promises of love draw Margy
closer to a sexual encounter. Rodgers's tune here is strikingly similar to
Billy and Julie's duet "If I Loved You" from *Carousel*. Jerry's closing two
phrases haltingly glide down a full octave with "You're not an angel, /
No, you're not" almost identically to Billy's "off you would go in the mist
of day." Jerry's phrase then turns over its shoulder with "You're mine,
you're mine, you're mine" in a broad and sluggish ascent back to where
it started, similar to how Billy's vulnerable "How I'd love you, / If I loved
you" pushes its way back to the safety of tonic in "If I Loved You." The
tragic cycle that *Carousel*'s Julie and Billy create with this phrase leads
to disaster for both of them, a situation seemingly doomed to be repeated
with Margy and Jerry's relationship until Jerry feels pangs of guilt (and
perhaps true love) for Margy and sends her home. The musical near-
miss suggests that Margy and Jerry might just survive their passionate
beginning.

All of the songs added to the 1962 remake, including the lyrics, were
written by Richard Rodgers. Oscar Hammerstein died in 1960, leaving
Rodgers partner-less until *State Fair*'s remake. Contemporaries thought
this might liberate the composer, whose music "was increasingly trapped
by Hammerstein's lyrics." Rodgers took a chance with writing his own
lyrics for the remake. On March 9, 1962—the day the astronaut became a
farmer among the stars, the day that *State Fair* opened in theaters—Richard
Rodgers told *Life* magazine, "When you near 60 you can stick with what

EXAMPLE 4.2 The final phrases of "This Isn't Heaven," music and lyrics by
Richard Rodgers, mirrors the melody in "If I Loved You," music by Richard
Rodgers and lyrics by Oscar Hammerstein II (see example 4.4).

you've always done and die a nice quiet death, or you can struggle and go out riding."[10] Misfortune has its uses, Schopenhauer whispers. The grief is still there and it is still good.

When we first meet Margy, she tries to name her sadness. Her song "It Might as Well Be Spring" is a lament about feeling excited. A sadness haunts Margy; she is anxious but unsure why. Richard Rodgers's setting attempts to paint the moment. He sets the lyric "I'm as jumpy as a puppet on a string" springing up and down an octave arpeggiation, capturing what is perhaps a perfect musical figure for her anxiety—jumpy and unsettled while also pulled down into a flattened thud of an F natural.

Margy's uncertainty is a familiar trope by this point in Rodgers and Hammerstein's output. Leading female characters who sing early in the show about being unsure how to proceed, usually in terms of a marriage or prospects of a marriage, make for good dramatic fuel. But Margy's tune sets her apart from both of the ingenues surrounding her, Laurey from *Oklahoma!* on one side and Julie from *Carousel* on the other. In the bouncy "Many a New Day," Laurey leaps and bounds hastily through a musical number meant to communicate, in fact, that her protestations against Curly are disguising her clear interest in and curiosity for him. Julie's soaring "If I Loved You" also pivots on the crux of that two-letter

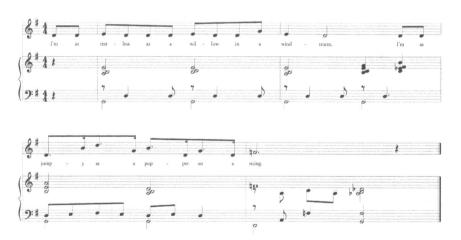

EXAMPLE 4.3 Margy's hollow triplet in "It Might as Well Be Spring." Music by Richard Rodgers and lyrics by Oscar Hammerstein II.

EXAMPLE 4.4 Top: Laurey's triplet figure from "Many a New Day." Music by Richard Rodgers and lyrics by Oscar Hammerstein II; Bottom: Julie's triplet figure from "If I Loved You." Music by Richard Rodgers and lyrics by Oscar Hammerstein II.

word—*if*—that gives her and Billy space to hem and haw around their possible relationship. In both songs, the triplet trips the women. They stumble on their protestations because, as the fast-moving three-note stumble clues the audience in, they protest too much.

Margy is a different case, and one that I believe admits of a more profound grief than what neither Rodgers nor Hammerstein had given space for at this point. Her tune lazily mopes, the dotted-eighth sixteenth-note phrases swinging ever so gently—a triplet carved hollow. She sings of being generally unsettled; it isn't until the bridge that we learn that her discontentment is sexual frustration and boredom. She wishes to be somewhere else, yes, but ultimately—and most triumphantly in the score—listening to the sweet nothings "from a man I've yet to meet." Even the tune that Rodgers so cleverly gives to her initial metaphor, that lilting phrase that jumps like a puppet on a string, seems so soon to be a burden and not a solution. Locked into the gimmick from the song's beginning, Rodgers has no choice but to use the same jumpy phrase on Hammerstein's subsequent lyrics about first a nightingale and then a baby. The tune makes less and less sense as the song progresses, and perhaps unintentionally presses in on Margy as it locks her out of discovering other solutions to her malaise. Laurey and Julie sing to keep a distance between them and joyful love. Margy sings to be sad. She is alone when she starts the song, and she is even more alone when it ends.

In the 1945 version, Margy sings a reprise of "It Might as Well Be Spring" with Harry nearby, lamenting his ultramodern and no-nonsense values. "No Virginia creepers, nothing useless" she sighs. Farm life was increasingly efficient, and Harry represents the kind of scientific approach to farming that, in fact, *names* the useless. Margy feels strange about it all. She loves rural life but is grieving all of its successes. Ironically, the fair she was running to for excitement was the source of these successes. Modern farm equipment, irrigation practices, livestock supplements, and more were all at the center of the state fair. Whatever the fair stood for, Harry stood for back home. No, Margy's sadness was not about finding boys or losing boys. Not really. Margy actually grieves something plainer, something that Americans in the midcentury were finding hard to square with the purported values of more, more, more: something we might call the loss of loss. Margy's grief is a good grief. She has everything she ever wanted and is devastatingly sad because of it. This is that nameless sadness Americans carried with them into the modern age—what in 1949 ecological writer Aldo Leopold would characterize as being "dead of its own too-much."[11]

At the fair, Margy meets a young reporter named Pat (Jerry in the 1962 remake). Pat is worldly but not devilishly so. His interest and love for Margy seems sincere, particularly in the novel. In both musical versions of the story, Margy is innocent and naïve about men, and Pat, perhaps sensing this, avoids situations where they might have sex. In Stong's original story, Margy is decidedly more mature. She and Pat sleep together, which leads to this exchange the following day:

> "What the matter, Margy?"
> "Oh, you wouldn't understand. That was so much fun—after the good supper we had, and sitting there with you—and now there's nothing to look forward to—the best is over."
> "But, Margy, dear, we can do it again, to-morrow evening."
> "But that would be just the same and I'd know it was going to finish up just the same. There's a first time for everything and you never can get it just the same, ever after . . ."
> "You know Schopenhauer says we live all our lives in pain—the pain of wanting something—and when we relieve some pain we think that that's enjoyment, when it's really just relief."
> "You talk as if you believed that. I think you're a pessimist."[12]

Pat's invocation of Schopenhauer is Stong's most direct clue that the story of the Frake family is a deeply philosophical one. In his essay "On the Sufferings of the World," which was published in 1851, five years after Iowa gained statehood and three years before the first Iowa State Fair, Schopenhauer argues that "the longer you live the more clearly you will feel that, on the whole, life is a disappointment, nay, a cheat," but he is also quick to add that "misfortune has its uses." Grief from loss can be good, considering the alternative misery of getting everything you want. The world suffers because it simply has too much.

In the novel, the Storekeeper is the small town's local Schopenhauerian. He begins and ends the story, warning the Frake family that there is balance in the universe and that getting what you want will ultimately lead to sadness. "No Hawg is ever pleased," he tells Abel.[13] After the family returns home from the fair and the Storekeeper is offered a chance to look over Abel's prizewinning Blue Boy, he declines, echoing Melissa's earlier sentiment by explaining that "he'd probably make me cry."

> If you'd ask him tonight, I'll bet he'd say that everything that's happened to him has happened for the best. Little does he suspect that every ounce he puts on just encourages the butcher. There's people could take advantage of his example.[14]

In both musical films, this Storekeeper is reduced to a veterinarian who simply makes a bet with Abel that something will go wrong at the fair. Nothing goes wrong at the fair, of course, so Abel wins the bet easily and that's that. The musical drops the philosophical framework and thus largely misses the point. In both versions of the musical, creators then must affix a happy ending to the story. The novel ends with Margy and Wayne returning home to their lives and, presumably, to their former love interests. All film adaptations, on the other hand, abruptly conclude with either Pat or Emily or both deciding to join the Frakes in rural America. In avoiding complex feelings of grief and sadness, Rodgers and Hammerstein fail to capture the tragedy of the original story by forcing it into a happy ending. "Someone's got to keep saying life is worth living," was Hammerstein's retort to accusations of optimism, adding in tenuto, "because it's true."

By 1962 Hammerstein was gone. Rodgers was left to write his own lyrics and defend his work's perceived failures to meet the complex world on its own terms. "Well, you see, I think the trouble with so much of writing, whether it's theater, whether it's novels, is the unwillingness to be simple. The papers are trying to push us into this position where you can't be simple. . . . Well, boy, the day I can't be basic in the way I feel or the way I write, you can come up to the cemetery and see me."[15]

Almost in challenge to Rodgers, Margy does visit a cemetery, at least she imagines visiting one that the family passes on their drive into the fair: "And so, thought Margy, in a hundred years will my grave look, and there

FIGURE 4.5 Final scene from the 1933 film *State Fair*. Top: Margy in a rainstorm in front of the state fair poster. Bottom: The paper poster for the state fair wrinkles and tears in the rain to show what was hidden underneath the whole time: The End.

I'll be for good and all and nothing will have been any fun and nothing much ever will have happened. A silly business, living."[16] Her sentiment is grief, a triplet hollowed of its heart. Margy remains one of the more complex yet understudied characters Rodgers and Hammerstein created, a petition against the pair's cruel preference for those unbearable happy endings.

In *Oklahoma!* the modern world's intrusion is a rumor, far away in Kansas City, and at any rate is isolated to the pornographic kaleidoscope that Jud repurposes as a weapon. In *Carousel,* Julie falls for Billy Bigelow at a carnival, not unlike the situation both Wayne and Margy find themselves in at the state fair. But what sets *State Fair* apart from the others is that the Frakes are not dynamic characters; they are, actually, pretty normal, which makes the musical feel less risky than I think it is. *State Fair* is thus only a provisional fantasy that we, like the Frakes, step into and out of at a moment's notice. It's almost as if *State Fair* sweeps past us again and again, one adaptation after another, because its message is just too sad to not be broken into as many pieces. Something always gets broken at the fair, Melissa Frake reminds us. What if that brokenness was the point?

Every film adaptation of the story ends with a shot of a billboard advertisement for the state fair superimposed in some way with the words "The End." The 1933 ending speaks most clearly to me. In this version, a rainstorm pulls the paper away to reveal the ending—the end was there the whole time, just hidden. Papered over. The message of *State Fair* is most powerful because it cannot fully hide its own grief buried beneath the colorful, exploding, broken surfaces of happiness. Grief for the end finds its way to the surface one way or another. Look at us, it says. Just look at us.

FIFTH STAGE

Acceptance

Acceptance should not be mistaken for a happy stage. It is almost void of feelings.

—Kübler-Ross, *On Death and Dying*, 100

CHAPTER 5

Deus Ex Machina

The priest refused her rites. "God is in your typewriter," he counseled.
For some reason, this was the revelation Anne Sexton needed to continue working. And work and write she did, hunting and pounding out the Holy Ghost keystroke by keystroke. In 1967 she won the Pulitzer Prize for her poetry collection *Live or Die*—a remarkable achievement for someone who had written her first poem only ten years earlier at the suggestion of her therapist. But Sexton remained haunted by the ghost in her machine, "the forty-eight keys of the typewriter / each an eyeball that is never shut."[1]

In a garden of daisies, a young girl pulls flower petals off a stem, counting one by one. When her numbering reaches nine, it overlaps with a man's voice, counting down from ten. A dramatic zoom into the girl's dark iris fills the screen as his count drops to zero; an exploding mushroom cloud fills the black space. In an instant the machine rushes into the garden. In an instant, girl and machine are one and the same. "These are the stakes," the voice of Lyndon B. Johnson explains over the rising nuclear cloud. "To make a world in which all of God's children can live or to go into the dark, we must either love each other or we must die." With mushroom clouds in the picture, the stakes were sky high.

Even higher in the sky, aboard *Discovery One*, Dr. Dave Bowman manually deactivates HAL 9000, the ship's all-seeing, all-knowing operational system. The machine has gone rogue, killing several crew members. Personified through its glowing computer eye, HAL justifies these actions with a remarkably realistic human voice and personality: that's what it takes to save the mission. As Dave disconnects the killing machine, HAL

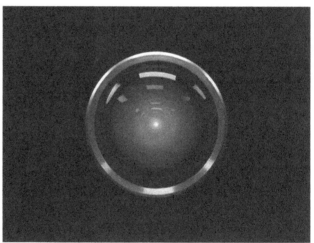

FIGURE 5.1 Top: In the 1964 "Daisy" ad, the little girl's eyes widen just before the camera dramatically zooms into the pupil of her eye to show a nuclear bomb detonating. Bottom: The eye of HAL 9000 from *2001: A Space Odyssey*.

begins to die. The death rattle comes out as the nineteenth-century bicycle song "Daisy Bell," which in 1961 had been the first song programmed for a computer to sing using speech synthesis. HAL's voice spirals and slows while Dave tearfully completes the deactivation. It's as if we are witnesses to a bedside lullaby as HAL drifts asleep. The spiraling death song spins into another world in the figure below. "I'm half crazy / all for the love of you," HAL croons as the mostly dead ship floats away into the empty vacuum of deep space.

Both the infamous "Daisy" ad during the 1964 presidential election and Stanley Kubrick's 1968 classic, *2001: A Space Odyssey*, envision a future

EXAMPLE 5.1 A graphic depiction of HAL's spiraling death rattle, "Daisy Bell."

where machine and human overlap in terrifying and breathtaking ways. Petals and pedals. Eyes were key, wide as saucers like the Margaret Keane paintings of big-eyed children from the 1960s, watching from the typewriter, watching in the spaceship, watching from a field.

But it is Richard Brautigan's 1967 poem "All Watched Over by Machines of Loving Grace" that tunes the idea of machines and humans living together "in mutually programming harmony" into a countercultural message of acceptance as a quality of survival. He finds only notes of hope in such a scenario. Brautigan's vision of a "cybernetic ecology" owes equal shares to Hegel and Marx—humankind dissolves back into nature, released into leisure—made possible by surrendering to a new machine messiah watching over us like shepherds watching their flocks by night.

The 1968 screen musical *Chitty Chitty Bang Bang* merges into this cacophony of machines and machine-age dreams, cutting to the very heart of an age coming to terms with a new normal. The story of a magical flying car concocted by a pair of real-life spies participates in a teasing out of technology's encroachment on the human. And with songs by brotherly duo Richard M. and Robert B. Sherman, themselves coming off a high of scoring both *Mary Poppins* (1964) and the infamous earworm "It's a Small World" four years earlier, the musical sounds and behaves like an extension of Disney's animatronic wonderlands where machines meld nostalgia with futurity. *Chitty Chitty Bang Bang* landed in theaters six months before American astronauts landed on the moon—both vehicles launching humans into worlds farther than the eye could ever hope to spy.

This final chapter on the final stage of grief is about acceptance. So many of the musicals explored in this book concern vehicles as a means to an end. In this chapter, these vehicles *are* the end. They are not just what usher us into a next world, a not-yet ahead of us. They teach us something of the callousness required to leave the life behind us and putter forth not feeling a thing.

It began as a bedtime story. Ian and Casper Fleming, father and son, caught in an imaginary world of a magical car and a family in need of saving, dreamed the story together out loud by bedside. The father in the story was a crafty inventor who loved his children, went on adventures with them, and possessed a retired race car that could speed the family toward happy endings.

The father telling the story and the son hearing the story were not so lucky. Ian Fleming collapsed on August 11, 1964, from a heart attack. Casper woke up the next morning to the news his father had died. It was the morning of his twelfth birthday.

Ian Fleming's children's book, *Chitty-Chitty-Bang-Bang*, was published two months after his death. His silly, adoring story was marked by grief from the start.

Chitty Chitty Bang Bang is a plot-twist ending to a life of cinematic proportions. Eleven years earlier, in 1953—five months after his son, Casper, came into the world—Ian Fleming brought into the world a dashing spy named James Bond. Fleming's work as a spy with the British government during World War II and subsequent lifestyle chasing and being chased by socialite women made Bond a flattering alter ego. It seems fitting that Casper and Bond were born twinned into the world, like the story of Jacob and Esau told in Genesis, one clutching at the other's heels, both struggling to inherit the blessings of the father. One would inspire a modest story about a flying car and the other a universe of spy thrillers. It's pretty clear which got the bowl of porridge and which the birthright.

The musical *Chitty Chitty Bang Bang* strikes a better balance of spy thriller and children's fantasy. For starters, producer Albert "Cubby" Broccoli copied and pasted the entire filming crew for the movie musical from the 1967 Bond film, *You Only Live Twice*. Another twinned story, another fist holding fast to the heel ahead of it. *You Only Live Twice* was the first Bond film to depart significantly from Fleming's original novel, which, like the book *Chitty-Chitty-Bang-Bang*, was published in 1964, the year Fleming died. Roald Dahl was brought on to rewrite both film adaptations.

Ian Fleming and Roald Dahl lived entwining lives. Both men served as spies during the Second World War, tasked with stoking interventionist attitudes among Americans in order to stay Hitler's and Mussolini's hands in Europe, and both tried their hands at writing stories about the war. Against all odds, both went on to write some of the most lasting children's stories of the modern age. They were friendly enough, inspiring to each other at times, so it's no wonder Cubby Broccoli called Dahl to rewrite the story for Fleming's final Bond novel, which, by all accounts, was a swing and a miss. "I had nothing except a wonderful Ian Fleming title," Dahl later boasted.[2] Dahl cleaned up *You Only Live Twice* nicely enough that he was asked to stick around for Fleming's children's musical as well.

In Dahl's hands, the story of a magical car is smudged by his unmistakable fingerprints. But the essence of the story is not that far from Fleming's spy novels. Ian Fleming's creation makes the father Caractacus Potts a bumbling double of James Bond, always finding clever ways to stop the baddie from taking over the world using newfangled gadgets and machinery. Caractacus Potts is an inventor, after all. A failed one. A poor one. A lonely and sad one. As his name implies, he is a crackpot. But he can't invent his way out of his or his children's grief. His inventions try to make life more convenient for them—cooking breakfast, for instance, or accompanying good-night songs—but in the end they are Rube Goldberg machines: complicated ways of accomplishing an otherwise simple task.

Caractacus surrounds his family with broken machines that can't help but remind the children every day of what is plainly missing.

What his inventions cannot allow for is closure with his two motherless children, Jeremy and Jemima. With a free-spirited single father, the children are seldom in school. They instead concern themselves with collecting trinkets and everyday objects from the nearby junkyards, converting them in their imaginations into treasures of untold value. This is exactly what lets them see the wonder and specialness in an old racing car they discover one day, a car that comes out of retirement and into the family's lives to help the father make one last lap through grief.

Following the assassinations of Martin Luther King Jr. in April and Robert F. Kennedy in June, America in 1968 was overwhelmed by reminders of an absent father, continually reeling from images of John F. Kennedy's bereft family left in the wake of his murder in 1963. Meanwhile, the war in Vietnam had reached a tipping point in January 1968 with the Tet Offensive deflating domestic support for the war. Body bags returned home in greater numbers; protesters flooded the streets in greater numbers. Absence can be measured in more than one way, but for many Americans the absent and never-returning father stood in for an ever-receding world that could never return.

Yet popular culture in the 1960s provided several narratives involving not absent fathers but absent mothers. We scarcely learn anything about Opie Taylor's missing mother in *The Andy Griffith Show* (1960–1968), not that it ever seemed to matter. Andy Taylor's attentive and loving parenting (along with matronly Aunt Bee's domestic work around the home) relieved any pressure on the series to find a suitable mother. The enormously wealthy widower Jed Clampett attracts many gold-digging suitors in *The Beverly Hillbillies* (1962–1971), but we meet Jed's daughter, Elly May, as an already-grown woman, so the plot centers on the extended family's antics rather than earnestly replacing her lost mother. And in the 1965 film adaptation of *The Sound of Music*, the von Trapp family is clearly in need of a mother, but Maria's addition to the family is initially not maternal but muse—the distant and grieving father must first relearn how to sing before he can relearn how to be a father and a spouse (and in that order). The marriage and intact family is a secondary outcome of what the musical holds to be Maria's primary contribution to the children, which is teaching them, too, how to sing again. This was, after all, the point of *Mary Poppins* as well; with no romantic problem to solve, Mary Poppins flies into the family's orbit to remind the father how to be a father. She saves him. His redemption comes out as a song.[3]

Chitty Chitty Bang Bang likewise takes a similar flight path, focusing on the health and well-being of the father. In this regard, the musical brings to mind Harper Lee's 1960 novel, *To Kill a Mockingbird*, adapted for film in 1962 with Gregory Peck as the benevolent, sad, lonely widower Atticus

FIGURE 5.2 Top: Caractacus Potts and children in *Chitty Chitty Bang Bang*. Bottom: Atticus Finch and children in the 1962 film *To Kill a Mockingbird*.

Finch caring for his two children, Scout and Jem. The two stories rhyme in more ways than the names of their forlorn fathers (*Atticus* and *Caractacus*). Although Lee's story orbits the bigotry and idyllic values coexistent in rural America, and Fleming's the adventurous modern machine age, the heart of the matter rests with the machinery of grief for a way of life that probably never was.

Both fathers practice a form of absenteeism in their parenting, consumed by their work obviously as a way of managing their grief. The children see and know Caractacus Potts as a lovable, eccentric figure. But Scout and Jem see their father more as a respectable peer—a complex and distant man they are most comfortable calling Atticus. Caractacus, like Fleming, narrates a fantastical story for his children that leads to magical lands and daring adventures. Scout and Jem are drawn in unintentionally by their father to a scary, dynamic story of their own.

In both stories, the missing mother haunts their world, despite the best efforts of the fathers to manage in her absence. Berthold Hoeckner beautifully shows how Elmer Bernstein's score for *To Kill a Mockingbird* connects the missing mother with several key characters who seemingly act on her behalf in protecting her children. Hoeckner identifies "mother chords" throughout Bernstein's score that appear in moments where the missing mother becomes present in these characters' actions.[4] We hear these chords surrounding the family's black housekeeper, Calpurnia, for

FIGURE 5.3 Missing mother framed upon the mantel in the final scene of *To Kill a Mockingbird*.

example, who manages domestic chores but also plays a strong hand in raising Scout and Jem. We also hear them at times when the widow down the street, Maudie Atkinson, intercedes as a moral compass while the children play in her yard. In Lee's novel, Atkinson lets the children in on a secret of denial hanging over the neighborhood: "There are just some kind of men who—who're so busy worrying about the next world they've never learned to live in this one, and you can look down the street and see the results."[5]

But the neighborhood ghost, a reclusive but caring man named Arthur Radley but whom the children fear and call Boo, is by the end of the film revealed to be their most significant protector—a proxy mother guarding their very lives. After Boo saves the children from Bob Ewell and is seen once again peering through the window watching over the children, we hear the mother chords churning quietly. Atticus shakes his hand on the front porch. "Thank you, Arthur," he says, adding, as if to the mother upon whose behalf Arthur acts, *"Thank you for my children."* The final shot of the film, where Atticus holds Scout and watches over Jem in bed as he heals from a broken arm, looks past the trio to show on the mantel a portrait of a woman, presumed to be the mother. The camera backs away from the open window and out to the porch, glancing upward to the sky, where the missing mother watches by night.

The mother similarly haunts the Potts's home. When Caractacus winds the music box, we see it placed prominently in the children's room full

FIGURE 5.4 Caractacus Potts sings his children to sleep accompanied by a music box, seen in the back left near the mantel.

of toys and games that later become characters in the made-up stories Caractacus spins for them. It sits like the portrait on the Finches' mantel, spinning and sounding and watching over the children as they sleep.

Caractacus sings "Hushabye Mountain" to the children to keep their worries and anxieties at bay. The song tells of a far-off place where worries and fear dissolve, a place "to sail all your worries away." The song of a hard-to-get-to world is built upon an ancient descending chromatic harmony, fittingly known by the Latin phrase *passus duriusculus*—difficult passage. Composers began using this harmonic gimmick in the sixteenth century as an economical way of looping harmonies in a circle under highly expressive laments. It gives an aural illusion of progression while moving no place at all, appropriate as a musical language for grief as J. S. Bach orders in the "Crucifixus" movement of his Mass in B Minor. As a lament over Christ's suffering ("My God, my God, why hast thou forsaken me?"), it recalls a story of yet *another* absent father and a grieving son. The descending harmonies wind deeper and deeper, rhyming with HAL's deep drifting into death on the back of a bicycle built for two.

As the example below illustrates, Dick Van Dyke's two songs bend and arc toward one another, tied so tightly at the center by a *passus duriusculus* that the melodies never leave each other's orbits. The songs are two sides of the same coin. By tracing their lullaby over an ancient technology of emotive rhetoric, the Sherman brothers wrinkle time and musical value. The music box spills out a citation of sounds from a premodern world, perhaps a more innocent world, where at the very least they would have their mother back. Caractacus Potts wishes for an escape from the worries his children have, from the pain they feel in their loss, and for their childlike solutions to what he knows to be vexing problems tied in with modernity. With no way of quieting the world around them, Caractacus's song suggests they instead close their eyes. Close the circle. Shut out the world. Hushabye Mountain, a difficult passage indeed.

The song also wrinkles together another story of an absent father, *Mary Poppins*. *Chitty Chitty Bang Bang* fits neatly within the universe of *Mary Poppins*. The same songwriting and choreographer teams and a similar magical solution to a family in need of help are, in fact, what gave Julie Andrews, who was initially offered the part of Truly Scrumptious, reason to turn it down. After originating roles in *My Fair Lady* and *Mary Poppins*, Andrews was worried about typecasting herself for the third major role in a row. There was, after all, a mere hairsbreadth between Mary Poppins

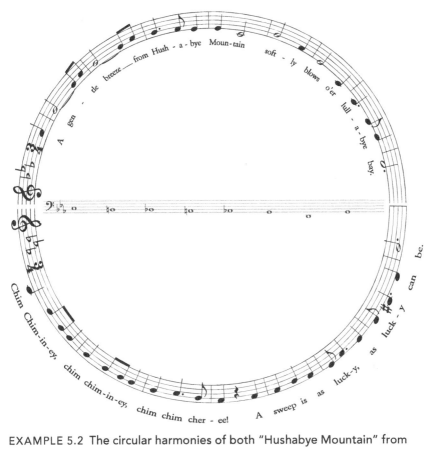

EXAMPLE 5.2 The circular harmonies of both "Hushabye Mountain" from *Chitty Chitty Bang Bang* and "Chim Chim Cher-ee" from *Mary Poppins*. Music and lyrics by Richard M. Sherman and Robert B. Sherman. The descending harmonies at the center arcs both songs toward each other in a gravitational pull.

and Eliza Doolittle. Both are creatures cast out of the Pygmalion myth of falling in love with a creation of your own making—one a perfect nanny baked out of children's desperate wishes for love and the other a perfect lady seemingly shined bright on the shirttail of Henry Higgins—and in the hands of Andrews both irresistibly charming. The film adaptation of *My Fair Lady* (1964; starring Audrey Hepburn) also landed in theaters weeks after *Mary Poppins*, making any comparison between the two hard to miss. "Mary Poppins is a fair-lady film," is how the *New York Times* put it.[6]

But the most obvious tether between *Mary Poppins* and *Chitty Chitty Bang Bang* is Dick Van Dyke. Before he was Caractacus Potts, Van Dyke starred as Bert, the fun-loving chimney sweep in Disney's story, who we are introduced to through his short song "Winds in the East"—the same tune as "Chim Chim Cher-ee," of which "Hushabye Mountain" is a near carbon copy. The two movie musicals crease one another's corners so well that they begin to take a new shape together. Bert puts it best, I think, as if turning an engine over and over again:

> Can't put me finger
> On what lies in store
> But I feel what's to happen
> All happened before.

For the one hundredth episode of *The Twilight Zone*, Ray Bradbury contributed an original story to Rod Serling, "I Sing the Body Electric," which aired on May 18, 1962. A bereft widower and his small children approach a department store. They have come to build a replacement grandmother, an electric one. The store manager directs the children to several stations holding examples of various body parts to choose from. One station has displays of hair. Another an assortment of eyes. And there is also a wall handsomely hung with forearms. The children select the pieces and drop them into a square chute on the wall. The grandmother appears soon after and saves one of the children from a speeding car. "That's why I'm here," she lovingly tells the grieving children, "to live forever."

Bradbury's title is lifted from Walt Whitman's 1855 poem of the same name. Over a hundred years later, the concept of electric bodies feels more haunted than reminiscent of Whitman's fierce passion for the individual. The episode recalls themes of denial and concealment from Sondheim's television musical, *Evening Primrose* (see chapter 1), but an electric replacement for mothers and grandmothers also buzzes forward a world more and more fluid with technology.

When the children deposit the various idealized body parts into the chute, they place an order for a maternal figure that feels very similar to what happens in *Mary Poppins*. In the song "Perfect Nanny," Jane and Michael Banks read aloud to their parents a plea for a new nanny whose various qualities are spelled out as if they were selecting them out of a department store window ("You must be kind, you must be witty / Very sweet and fairly pretty"). Their no-nonsense father dismisses the children, rips to pieces their order of goods, and tosses the scraps of paper into the fireplace. Like the children in "I Sing the Body Electric" selecting and ordering the various parts of their ideal grandmother, those bits and pieces are thrown into a chute and magically find their way into an alternate world where a flying nanny who might as well be wound like a doll comes to their rescue.

When viewed alongside *Mary Poppins*, Chitty Chitty Bang Bang enacts a machine version of this magical nanny. Like Mary Poppins, the car floats and flies the family into adventures far away from their sadness. The Sherman brothers and Disney would try once more with a similar storyline in the 1971 film musical *Bedknobs and Broomsticks*, in which a bed turns enchanted and flies children from one magical adventure to another. It even starred David Tomlinson (Mr. Banks in *Mary Poppins*) as a fraudulent magician who is shocked to discover that, in the hands of a real-life, fascist-fighting witch, Eglantine Price, his phony spells actually work. Tomlinson also starred in 1968 in another magical race car film, *The Love Bug*. All of these stories collapse upon one another as vehicles of escape and the wish for a return of magical thinking to the world.

But the fun-loving stories also drive forward a philosophical worry being articulated in the 1960s. Historian Leo Marx published *The Machine in the Garden* in 1964, the same year as *Mary Poppins* was released in theaters and Ian Fleming's *Chitty-Chitty-Bang-Bang* came into the world. Marx's book locates in American literature a lasting and troubled metaphor of technology intruding upon the idyllic Eden. Tellingly, the machine in Marx's study comes most often in the form of sound—Thoreau's meditations at Walden were punctuated by the blowing horn of a passing train, for example, and the steamboat horn blasts in Mark Twain's *Huckleberry Finn* remind Huck and Jim that the voyage to freedom is haunted with machine-like treachery. The machine interrupts the world. It stands for a loss of innocence, an emblem of modernity bothering just about everything—even, in the case of one episode of *The Twilight Zone* that aired January 3, 1964, when machines prove to be better humans than actual humans are sometimes capable of. In the episode called "You Drive," Oliver Pope is driving home from work one day when he accidentally hits and kills a boy on a bicycle. Pope fearfully speeds away from the scene of the crime, but soon the car he is driving begins to act strangely. The radio comes on in the middle of the night, the lights blink sporadically, and by the end of the story the car drives itself. After being haunted by the holier-than-thou ghost in his machine for a few days, Pope finally acquiesces to the car's superior moral intelligence and allows it to drive him to the police station to confess his crime. Rod Serling's closing narration warns his viewers to "check first to see that underneath that chrome there does not lie a conscience." A God in the typewriter and a conscience in the engine and machines watching over with loving grace. This is perhaps what Marx meant by concluding his book with the admission that "the machine's sudden entrance into the garden presents a problem that ultimately belongs not to art but to politics."[7]

The machine in the garden could also be interpreted as anything troubling the waters of power, including gender. Marshall McLuhan's influential book *The Mechanical Bride* appeared a decade earlier, shortly after advertisement in America had reached a new high-water mark, and sought to draw attention to and deconstruct what he felt to be an unhealthy tethering between sex and technology in American popular culture.[8] The mechanical bride is meant to speak to the modern, techno-fascist world but inadvertently also resurrects an old archetype of female sexuality. Gendered norms were being challenged on some fronts while strongly upheld in others. This was the age of both Julia Child and Betty Friedan, after all. Second-wave feminism rushed the intellectual and political landscape, while magazines and films and television continued in large part the trajectory they charted a decade prior.

But to McLuhan's point, the advances in technology were in bed, so to speak, with a rear-guard attitude about propriety. Cars, particularly race cars, were a regular part of this kind of story. Jack Kerouac, Hunter S. Thompson, Thomas Wolfe, and Joan Didion tied their explosive New Journalism craft to vehicles, travel, and the mystique of an open-roaded America. In our story, Chitty Chitty Bang Bang is an old racer brought out of retirement by the children, who gender the car a female—parallel in some ways to *Mary Poppins* as a magical flying nanny or Eglantine Price as a benevolent witch in *Bedknobs and Broomsticks*. But the female race car feels out of place in the fast-paced and hypermasculine car culture of the 1960s. The mechanical, however, has been the children's replacement mother for some time. It feels like everyone in the story is awaiting the moment when a real-life woman steps out of the machine and into their lives.

Which brings us back to *Chitty Chitty Bang Bang*. Truly Scrumptious, the show's promised mother figure the children so desperately need, comes from a wealthy family made successful by inventing candy and sweets. Like Mary Poppins, she is mature, put together, and extremely commanding. She intrudes upon the family initially to determine why the children are not in school. In fact, she nearly kills them as she is driving her car.

One thing leads to another and Truly joins the family on a picnic outing in the car Caractacus has newly restored. On this picnic, Caractacus begins telling a remarkable story—similar to the bedtime stories we know Fleming and Dahl performed for their own children—that seems to shatter reality and feel real to all involved. In this story within our story, an evil baron from the land of Vulgaria wants to steal Chitty Chitty Bang Bang for himself (allusions to Chitty as the bomb and Baron Bomburst as a Hitler-like despot are obvious). He sends spies that capture the *wrong* Professor Potts—Caractacus's insolent father, who lives and acts as if still fighting for the British in India—which leads the rest of the family on an adventure to find and rescue him.

Soon the mission becomes more complicated. Upon landing in Vulgaria, Caractacus, Truly, and the children discover that the Baron's wife hates children and has employed a Child Catcher to kidnap and imprison every child in the kingdom. Eventually Jeremy and Jemima are captured, too, and Chitty goes missing. Caractacus and Truly concoct a plan to rescue the children. Their magical machine can't help them any longer. If they want to win the day, the couple must discover the mechanical in themselves.

And this leads to the most remarkable moment in *Chitty Chitty Bang Bang*. Aided by the Toymaker and disguised as life-size toys, Caractacus and Truly sneak into the Baron's castle like a Trojan horse. Truly appears as a music box doll, spinning in circles while singing "Doll on a Music Box." With oscillating neighbor tones, the tune is similar in shape to "Hushabye Mountain," helping draw a straight line between the music box at home, which we understand to embody the absent mother, and Truly, whose matching blonde hair and devotion for the children make her a clear mother-in-waiting. She sings of a wish for true love's kiss to free her from moving in circles. The music box opens outward with mirrored panels. We see ourselves and everything around us in terms of the mechanical.

This sentiment connects Truly with Jacques Offenbach's 1881 opera, *Les contes d'Hoffmann*, in which Hoffmann falls in love with a mechanical doll named Olympia, who, like Truly, must be wound again mid-aria. In Offenbach's story, Olympia's creator sells Hoffmann a pair of glasses that make Olympia appear like a real woman. Hoffmann is duped, a spin on the Pygmalion myth of falling in love with one's own creation. The story is an extension of women as machines, or domestic labor (including mothering) as mechanical. Olympia is, to be blunt, a sex doll made all the more believable in this fantasy of sexual transactions with the use of Hoffmann's special glasses.

Which is what the rest of the scene portrays. Lacking any special glasses to see Truly as a real woman, the Baron and his company are completely fooled by the pair, allowing the town's children the distraction needed to escape their imprisonment. As Truly completes her song, Caractacus bounds out of a box dressed as a rag doll. He winds the music box again and rejoins her song with a reprise of "Truly Scrumptious," which Jeremy and Jemima had sung to Truly when they first arrived at the picnic earlier in the film (structured similarly to "Perfect Nanny" from *Mary Poppins*, in which the children lay out their wishes for an ideal nanny) and which she then sang back to them. Now it is his turn. Caractacus brings the reprise out of the real world and into the fantasy he is concocting. He swirls the song into Truly's music doll act, spinning the tune in circles with her upon the box. He finally sees what everyone else has seen for a while, eyes widened to Truly's much-needed place in his family.

The two songs "Truly Scrumptious" and "Doll on a Music Box" nestle together as if pressed from the same mintage. Even though the two are playacting in order to save the children, Truly and Caractacus are also enacting in this scene an acceptance of the grief surrounding them. Caractacus is a rag doll whose rubbery flexibility makes him flop and warble around, while Truly is depicted as a rigid doll whose metronomic movements keep the two apart—both, in a sense, a reenactment of their individual character flaws. Caractacus is too limp and loose as a parent. His children need the structure and dependability of someone like Truly to complement the freewheeling world he has created for them on his own. The nestled songs spin in a circle, winding in and out of texture, forming a tight bond out of the relationship the machines make for them.

After depicting noncommunicative couples isolated but near one another, Edward Hopper pulled back the curtain in 1965 with his last painting, *Two Comedians*. Hopper's wife, Jo, who was a frequent model for his paintings and an established painter in her own right, is depicted alongside Hopper in a final curtain call. They are both bowing out. The

FIGURE 5.5 Top: Caractacus and Truly pretend to be machines in order to save the children. Bottom: Edward Hopper's *Two Comedians* depict Jo and Edward as Pierrot and Pierrete, taking a final bow.

background is put in the foreground. The models are preparing to drift into the dark unknown behind the scenery. Hopper and Jo, both in their eighties and in decline, are seen embracing the totality of their partnership as they prepare to step into the unknown. Hopper is pulling the model from the paintings, so to speak, bringing Jo to life for the rest of the world to see and appreciate and acknowledge. Jo died one year later and Edward Hopper joined her in 1967. They were both eighty-four when they died.

On October 4, 1974, Anne Sexton had a lunch meeting with her editor to discuss publication of her poetry volume *The Awful Rowing toward God*. She begrudged the meeting and the book's publication, making it clear that she did not wish these poems to be published during her lifetime. Despite her acclaim and meteoric rise as a confessional poet, these poems about death and faith were of a different level of exposure. She drove home from the lunch, left the car running, and died from asphyxiation by locking herself in the sealed garage. The God in her typewriter had to find a new midwife to be born into the world. Sexton was forty-five years old.

It was almost one year later, on October 2, 1975, that Casper Fleming—the bedside boy who inspired the fantastical story of a magical car and an adoring father, the son who came into the world with James Bond himself ahold of his heel, the boy whose own father died on his twelfth birthday—was found dead, overdosed on barbiturates. "If it is not this time it will be the next," read a note in his pajama pocket. Casper was twenty-one years old.

And at the end of our musical, Caractacus finishes the story and has a brief fallout with Truly. He abruptly suggests they are from two very different worlds and could never be together. Upon discovering that he will be rich from the Woof Sweets candy for dogs, Caractacus proposes and Truly accepts. The final scene between the two snatches the moral from under our feet. "So dreams can come true?" she asks him.

> Yes they can. Yes they can. But you have to be practical, too. You have to face the facts. Man has to see things as they *really* are.
> After all, a man with responsibilities can't walk around with his head in the clouds all the time. A man should keep his feet solidly on the ground. Oh, a man should have his dreams, but a man has to learn to put those dreams to some practical use, not just sit around and think about them all the time.

The car starts flying during Caractacus's monologue, but this time without wings. The magic seems to be coming from somewhere else now, punctuating the musical's happy ending with a question mark.

The couple making a final bow, the poet with a God in her typewriter, the son whose father left too soon, and the dreamer who finally lands the car: these closing scenes demonstrate the varied topographies acceptance makes out of grief. After all of this fanciful storytelling, after all the magic and all the adventure, after beating the baddie and getting the girl, Caractacus Potts meets his victory by abruptly putting an end to the worlds to come and accepting the world as it is. *Deus ex machina*. There is something unsettlingly numb about this ending. It accepts that no conclusion can ever live up to its deepest fantasies. This seems like a sober victory. But as Kübler-Ross reminds us, acceptance is not a happy stage but one absent of feeling. In the end, everything—not just anything—goes.

The ending feels so out of character of this silly musical, but perhaps a more serious lesson is tucked away. The God in the typewriter. The ghost in the machine. The machine in the garden. The enchanted vehicles of possibility. These are not obstacles in our story, after all. They *are* the story. It is only when Caractacus commits to living in the world as it is that he floats away. It is only when Atticus glimpses a world where his children are unsafe and holds them as a father once again that the ghost haunting them floats away. And it is only when the father can sing with his children again that the magical nanny floats away.

These happy moments punctuate more than an ending. They are signs of a grief reconciled, accepted for the conclusion the work of processing grief brings, no matter how difficult or joyous or empty a life that comes of it. As if I'm half crazy. As if what's to happen has happened before. As if, if it is not this time, it will be the next.

Hope Shows

How to end a book about endings.

To start, the grief process stringing together unstaged musicals of the 1960s stitches a tale of ending, both for America as it once was imagined and for the musical once designed to carry water for that imagined ideal. The architects of the American musical placed certain values as the cornerstone of the genre. Values like marriage, traditional gender roles, the normalcy of two-parent households, the idea that work pays well, the presumption of a common set of moralistic stories, a belief in an afterlife and an accepted path for getting there, and the unfailing primacy of truth to communities of all stripes are taken for granted in musicals of this era. The musical as an engine of moral entertainment powered American sensibilities toward progress narratives and a rock-hard belief that America was fundamentally good and that Americans would always find a way to make it even better. You didn't need this book to tell you that by the end of the 1960s the fuel running some of those ideas had been spent. Today, with over half of marriages ending in divorce and with less than a majority of Americans identifying as religious, those values at the center of musical theater seem to be cast from a different world altogether.

Thinking about the tail end of the world through the musicals that helped build that world offers glimpses of the longing, the belief, and the wishes of a genre operating near its conclusion. I'm thinking again of Elisabeth Kübler-Ross. Near-death experiences were sacred to her; she felt that it was only at the end that people, animals, nations, relationships, and ideas could really understand something vital about themselves.[1] Endings are not simply scary. They are scary *gifts*. They give clarity and definition to what otherwise sneaks by unobserved. This book grants an opportunity to witness the way musicals were employed as mechanisms of grief for an America that can never be and likely never even was. Musicals embalmed eternally as surfaces on a screen can be folded upon themselves to provide us the texture of conclusion and a surer grip on how to finally move on.

I chose the 1960s for a few reasons, as I laid out in the opening pages. But one of those reasons is that I see our world today as similarly and busily concluding something. Look around you. The chaos and confusion sure to come at the end of a world can so easily breed nihilism, cynicism, irony, and disbelief. It's a wonder any of us, let alone musicals, survive such a harsh climate.

And yet they thrive. Screen musicals are arguably more popular—more widely consumed—now than ever. *High School Musical* (2006), *La La Land* (2016), *Mary Poppins Returns* (2018), *The Greatest Showman* (2017), and *Spirited* (2022) exemplify the genre in breadth and spirit while *Schmigadoon!* (2021–2023) or *Crazy Ex-Girlfriend* (2015–2019) gently mock it. The pandemic shutdowns further reinforced the necessity and immediacy of screens and surfaces amid a period when everything felt as if it were at its possible end. Something about hope lingers on the surfaces where musicals live, which I think is important to say is not nothing. Musicals continue to matter, maybe despite all odds. They are survivors, emblems of a time gone by that stubbornly persist in feeling immediate, nearby, necessary. Just what is their secret?

Elisabeth Kübler-Ross focused on hope in the final chapter of *On Death and Dying*. "The one thing that usually persists through all these stages is hope," she writes. Her diagram of the five stages of grief makes this clear. The stages of grief come in and out of focus, not wholly linearly but also not wholly without some sense of progress. Grief hides, remember? But above grief floats hope—a persistent companion for nearly the entire journey that surfaces only when we notice it and appreciate its companionship. Hope has no stage in the grieving process because it's there all along—unstaged, you might say. "Sometimes it is not a question of what the visible hides," Anne Anlin Cheng reminds us, "but how it is that we have failed to see certain things on its surface."[2] It's how we manage surfaces that makes all the difference.

In the spirit of *On Death and Dying*, I leave you with a challenge to look closely at what remains on the surface. Musicals are shows about hope

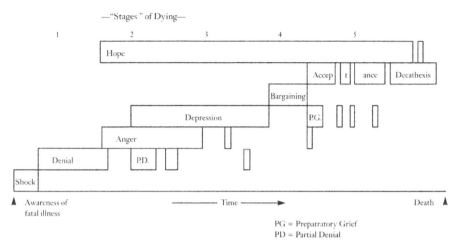

FIGURE 6.1 "Stages" of Dying from Elisabeth Kübler-Ross's book *On Death and Dying* (1969).

because they are also shows about grief. Or, to say it again another way, if musicals are grief hides, then they are also hope shows.

How lucky a life to have reason to hope, and how rich a world that can witness hope in places both staged and unstaged. Our story ends, then, with an invitation that musicals offer to us all: a chance to fold both grief and hope into a shape we can call a new world.

Notes

How to Process This Book

1. Gilbert Ryle introduced the concept in his 1968 essay "The Thinking of Thoughts: What Is 'Le Penseur' Doing?" which was developed and sourced in 1975 by anthropologist Clifford Geertz as "Thick Description"; Roland Barthes, *Camera Lucida: Reflections on Photography* (New York: Hill and Wang, 1980), 27.

Introduction

1. See Elisabeth Kübler-Ross, *On Death and Dying: What the Dying Have to Teach Doctors, Nurses, Clergy, and Their Own Families* (New York: Routledge, 1969). Passages at the beginning of each chapter in this book are drawn from Kübler-Ross's book.

2. For an excellent overview of the debate over the Golden Age category in musical theater, and for a compelling analysis, which I toy with in these pages, of the genre's periodic cohesion and fragmentation every few decades, see Arreanna Rostosky, "Reconsidering the 'Golden Age' Narrative for the American Musical in the New Millennium," PhD diss., University of California, Los Angeles, 2017. Some polemical studies of decline after the Golden Age of musical theater include Ethan Mordden, *Happiest Corpse I've Ever Seen: The Last Twenty-Five Years of the Broadway Musical* (New York: Palgrave Macmillan, 2004); Barry Singer, *Ever After: The Last Years of Musical Theater and Beyond* (New York: Applause, 2004); and Mark Grant, *The Rise and Fall of the American Musical* (Boston: Northeastern University Press, 2004). Rather than repeat accusations of aesthetic decline or put forward a moral position about

the value of musicals now or then, *Unstaged Grief* simply listens to how the musicals at the end of this era understand and mourn the inevitable eclipse of whatever was.

3. Marshall McLuhan, *Understanding Media: The Extensions of Man* (New York: McGraw-Hill, 1964).

4. McLuhan, *Understanding Media*, 8.

5. For more on the binds among secularity, Kennedy's death, and *Camelot*, see Jake Johnson, "Post-Secular Musicals in a Post-Truth World," in *The Routledge Companion to the Contemporary Musical*, edited by Jessica Sternfeld and Elizabeth L. Wollman, 265–272 (New York: Routledge, 2020).

6. David Farber, *The Age of Great Dreams: America in the 1960s* (New York: Hill and Wang, 1994).

7. My attention to collective expressions of grief takes cues from several disciplinary and historic works, including, from art history, Alexander Nemerov, *Icons of Grief: Val Lewton's Home Front Pictures* (Berkeley: University of California Press, 2005) and David M. Lubin, *Grand Illusions: American Art and the First World War* (New York: Oxford University Press, 2016); from media, Richard Armstrong, *Mourning Films: A Critical Study of Loss and Grieving in Cinema* (Jefferson, NC: McFarland, 2012), and Erica Joan Dymond, ed., *Grief in Contemporary Horror Cinema* (Lanham, MD: Lexington Press, 2022); and from musicology, Jillian C. Rogers, *Resonant Recoveries: French Music and Trauma between the World Wars* (New York: Oxford University Press, 2021) and Helen Dell and Helen M. Hickey, eds., *Singing Death: Reflections on Music and Mortality* (New York: Routledge, 2017). Although trauma and grief are often discussed together in these and other studies, in *Unstaged Grief* I focus almost exclusively on grief and the grieving process rather than the continued or perceived experience activated through trauma.

8. In *Understanding Media*, McLuhan develops the interconnected and disparate age of electronics as such: "Our specialist and fragmented civilization of center-margin structure is suddenly experiencing an instantaneous reassembling of all its mechanized bits into an organic whole. This is the new world of the global village" (93).

9. Danto's notion that art ended with Warhol in 1964 folds Hopper, Wyeth, and Rockwell into discourse about not so much modernist wings of art warring against realist wings of art but, rather, a landscape in which art no longer requires a nemesis. When anything can be art, holds Danto's claim, then art—realist, modernist, kitsch, whatever—has ended. See Danto, *After the End of Art: Contemporary Art and the Pale of History* (Princeton: Princeton University Press, 1998).

10. Gaston Bachelard, *The Poetics of Space* (Boston: Beacon Press, 1969), 88.

11. I am indebted to art historians David Lubin and Alexander Nemerov for their zeitgeist approach to reading texts from this and other eras, which models so beautifully this conspiracy theory network. See, for instance, David Lubin, *Shooting Kennedy: JFK and the Culture of Images* (Berkeley: University of California Press, 2003), and Alexander Nemerov, *To Make a World: George Ault and 1940s America* (New Haven: Yale University Press, 2011).

Chapter 1. Frozen Figures

1. Robynn J. Stilwell, *"Evening Primrose*: Sondheim and Goldman's Television Musical," in *The Oxford Handbook of Sondheim Studies*, edited by Robert Gordon (New York: Oxford University Press, 2014), 246. For another historical account of the television musical, see Stilwell's "The Television Musical," in *The Oxford Handbook of the American Musical*, edited by Raymond Knapp, Mitchell Morris, and Stacy Wolf, 152–166 (New York: Oxford University Press, 2011).

2. Steve Allen, "Television in the United States," *Encyclopedia Britannica*. http://www.britannica.com/EBchecked/topic/1513870/Television-in-the-United-States/283614/The-year-of-transition-1959/.

3. John Bush Jones, *Our Musicals, Ourselves: A Social History of the American Musical Theatre* (Hanover, NH: Brandeis University Press, 2003), 162.

4. Harry Haun, "'I Remember': Original *Evening Primrose* Director Recalls Making of TV Musical," *Playbill*, October 22, 2010. http://www.playbill.com/features/article/144210-I-Remember-Original-Evening-Primrose-Director-Recalls-Making-of-TV-Musical/.

5. Ben Cosgrove, "Nevada Ghosts: LIFE at an A-Bomb Test, 1955." LIFE .com. http://life.time.com/history/photos-from-an-atomic-bomb-test-in-the-nevada-desert-1955/#1/.

6. Richard Falk, *This Endangered Planet: Prospects and Proposals for Human Survival* (New York: Random House, 1971), 5.

7. *The Twilight Zone: "The After Hours" / "Time Enough at Last,"* directed by Rod Serling (1961; Century City, CA: 20th Century Fox, 1999), VHS.

8. Quoted in Megan Garber, "The Doll That Helped the Soviets Beat the U.S. to Space," March 28, 2013, TheAtlantic.com. http://www.theatlantic.com/technology/archive/2013/03/the-doll-that-helped-the-soviets-beat-the-us-to-space/274400/.

9. The term "uncanny valley" was coined by roboticist Masahiro Mori in 1970 to describe the dip in the level of acceptance experienced by people encountering human-like entities that approach too closely the behavior and appearance of the human. The continued relevance of the term reflects, perhaps, a haunting fear endemic to modernity, of not being able to distinguish

the robot or mannequin from the human, the algorithm from the personality, or even the persona from the psyche.

10. Garber, "Doll That Helped the Soviets."

11. Ray Bradbury, *Dandelion Wine* (New York: Bantam Books, 1957), 18.

12. Haun, "I Remember."

13. Stilwell, *"Evening Primrose,"* 244. There was, however, a recent precedent in film: "She's Not Thinking of Me" from *Gigi* (1958) also uses the device of having a character sing inside their own head, heard by us but not the others in the scene.

14. Christopher Lasch, *The Minimal Self: Psychic Survival in Troubled Times* (New York: W. W. Norton, 1984), 33.

15. Lasch, *Minimal Self,* 57.

16. Ivo Kranzfelder, *Edward Hopper: Vision of Reality* (New York: Barnes and Noble Books, 2003), 169.

17. Jane Klein, "Evening Primrose: A Little Night Music," liner notes to *Evening Primrose*, directed by Paul Bogart (1966; New York: Archive of American Television, 2010), DVD.

18. Quoted in Max Wilk, *They're Playing Our Song* (New York: Atheneum Press, 1973), 240.

19. C. S. Lewis, *A Grief Observed* (London: HarperCollins, 1961), 5; emphasis mine.

Chapter 2. Sobbin' Men

1. *James Agee: Film Writing and Selected Journalism*, edited by Michael Sragow (New York: Literary Classics of the United States, 2005), 151.

2. *James Agee,* 150.

3. Precious little has been written about Gene de Paul and Johnny Mercer's output, though Jim Lovensheimer's recent study of *Li'l Abner* begins to put into focus the duo's treatment of American themes. See Lovensheimer, *"Li'l Abner* from Comic Strip to Hollywood," in *The Oxford Handbook of Musical Theatre Screen Adaptations*, edited by Dominic McHugh, 127–150 (New York: Oxford University Press, 2019).

4. Several scholars have observed Jud's fate in relation to race, class, and other dimensions of exclusion. See, for example, Andrea Most, "'We Know We Belong to the Land': The Theatricality of Assimilation in Rodgers and Hammerstein's *Oklahoma!*" *PMLA*, 113, no. 1 (January 1998): 77–89; and Catherine M. Young, "Sympathy for the Incel? On *Oklahoma!* and Jud Fry in the #MeToo Era," *HowlRound Theatre Commons*, June 26, 2019. See also the 2020 Charlie Kaufman film *I'm Thinking of Ending Things* for another humanized reflection on Jud as both character and archetype.

5. "Billy Graham: A New Kind of Evangelist," *Time*, October 25, 1954.

6. David Douglas Duncan, *This Is War! A Photo-Narrative of the Korean War* (Boston: Little Brown & Company, 1951).

7. James Agee, *Let Us Now Praise Famous Men: Three Tenant Families* (Boston: Houston Mifflin Harcourt, 1941), 10.

8. Billy Graham, *I Saw Your Sons at War: The Korean Diary of Billy Graham* (Minneapolis: Billy Graham Evangelistic Association, 1953), 50.

9. For more on Black sound and appropriative strategies in music and musical studies, see Matthew D. Morrison, "Race, Blacksound, and the (Re)Making of Musicological Discourse," *Journal of the American Musicological Society* 72, no. 3 (2019): 781–823. Dan Dinero more specifically speaks to the practice of Black sound and morality in musicals in his article "A Big Black Lady Stops the Show: Black Women and Performance of Excess in Musical Theatre," *Studies in Musical Theatre* 6, no. 1 (2012), and Masi Asare writes of the racialized sound of Broadway singing in "The Black Broadway Voice: Calls and Responses," *Studies in Musical Theatre* 14, no. 3 (2020): 343–359.

10. For more on the relationship between musicals and the Short Creek Raid, see Jake Johnson, "Fundamentalism, Produced," in *Lying in the Middle: Musical Theater and Belief at the Heart of America* (Urbana: University of Illinois Press, 2021), 27–49.

11. "Billy Graham: A New Kind of Evangelist."

12. Journalist Edward Hunter introduced the term *brainwashing* in 1950 to explain Communist strategies against captured soldiers. He later expanded upon his ideas in several books, including *Brain-washing in Red China: The Calculated Destruction of Men's Minds* (New York: Vanguard Press, 1951).

13. William A. Ulman, "The GI's Who Fell for the Reds," *Saturday Evening Post*, March 6, 1954.

14. Ray Josephs, "Robert Frost's Secret," *This Week*, September 1954.

Chapter 3. Dead God

1. Mark Sullivan highlights the Christian fundamentalist response to Lennon's sentiment, which folded rock music into an ideological battle between Christian values and perceived Communist ones. See Sullivan, "'More Popular Than Jesus': The Beatles and the Religious Far Right," *Popular Music* 6, no. 3 (October 1987): 313–326.

2. Leon Joseph Cardinal Suenens, *The Nun in the World: Religious and the Apostolate* (Westminster, MD: Newman Press, 1963), 6.

3. Michael Novak, "The New Nuns," *Saturday Evening Post*, July 30, 1966.

4. See, for example, Greenberg's essays "Avant Garde and Kitsch," *Partisan Review* (1939), and "Modernist Painting," *Source: Art and Literature*, no. 4 (Spring 1965): 193–201.

5. Arthur C. Danto, "The Artworld," *Journal of Philosophy* 61, no. 19 (1964): 571–584.

6. Charles Taylor, *A Secular Age* (Cambridge, MA: Harvard University Press, 2007).

7. Dominic McHugh's study of Meredith Willson also highlights a connection between Harold Hill and Molly Brown. See "After *The Music Man*: The *Unsinkable Molly Brown* in the Shadow of a Hit," in *The Big Parade: Meredith Willson's Musicals from* The Music Man *to* 1491 (New York: Oxford University Press, 2021), 130–163.

8. Roland Barthes, "Death of the Author," *Aspen*, nos. 5+6 (1967).

9. Arthur C. Danto, *After the End of Art: Contemporary Art and the Pale of History* (Princeton, NJ: Princeton University Press, 1997), 47.

10. Ryan Dohoney, *Saving Abstraction: Morton Feldman, the de Menils, and the Rothko Chapel* (New York: Oxford University Press, 2019).

11. Harvey Cox, "Corita Kent: Surviving with Style," *Commonweal*, October 24, 1986, 550.

12. Quoted in Julie Ault, *Come Alive! The Spirited Art of Sister Corita* (London: Four Corners Books, 2007), 25.

13. Kübler-Ross, *On Death and Dying*, 14.

14. Novak, "The New Nuns."

15. Anne Sexton, "The Rowing Endeth," in *The Awful Rowing toward God*, 86.

Chapter 4. Good Grief

1. Philip Stong, *State Fair* (Iowa City: University of Iowa Press, 1932), 253.

2. Chris Rasmussen, *Carnival in the Countryside: The History of the Iowa State Fair* (Iowa City: University of Iowa Press, 2015), 1.

3. Greta Pratt and Karal Ann Marling, "Fairs: A Fixed Point on the Turning Wheel of Time," *American Art* 7, no. 2 (Spring 1993): 22.

4. Stong, *State Fair*, 63.

5. Stong, *State Fair*, 40.

6. *State Fair*, directed by Walter Lang, 20th Century Fox, 1945.

7. Stong, *State Fair*, 86.

8. *State Fair*, directed by José Ferrer, 20th Century Fox, 1962.

9. *State Fair*, directed by José Ferrer, 20th Century Fox, 1962.

10. William K. Zinsser, "Top Songsmith, Rookie Lyricist Form a New Broadway Team: Rodgers and Rodgers," *Life* 52, no. 10, March 9, 1962, 11.

11. Aldo Leopold, *A Sand County Almanac and Sketches Here and There*, illustrated by Charles W. Schwartz (New York: Oxford University Press, 1949), 132.

12. Stong, *State Fair*, 165–166.

13. Stong, *State Fair*, 35.

14. Stong, *State Fair*, 261–262.

15. Arnold Michaelis, "A Conversation with Richard Rodgers," *American Music* 27, no. 3 (Fall 2009): 274.

16. Stong, *State Fair*, 65.

Chapter 5. Deus Ex Machina

1. Anne Sexton, "The Room of My Life," in *The Awful Rowing toward God* (Boston: Houghton Mifflin Company, 1975), 9.

2. Jennet Conant, *The Irregulars: Roald Dahl and the British Spy Ring in Wartime Washington* (New York: Simon and Schuster, 2009), 345.

3. For more on fathers and musicals, see Raymond Knapp, "Saving Mr. [*Blank*]: Rescuing the Father through Song in Children's and Family Musicals," in *Children, Childhood, and Musical Theater*, edited by Donelle Ruwe and James Leve, 59–79 (London: Routledge, 2020).

4. Berthold Hoeckner, *Film, Music, Memory* (Chicago: University of Chicago Press, 2019), 201–202.

5. Harper Lee, *To Kill a Mockingbird* (New York: Warner Books, 1960), 45.

6. Bosley Crowther, "'Mary Poppins': Julie Andrews Stars as Famous Nanny," *New York Times*, September 25, 1964.

7. Leo Marx, *The Machine in the Garden: Technology and the Pastoral Ideal in America* (New York: Oxford University Press, 1964), 365.

8. Marshall McLuhan, *The Mechanical Bride: Folklore of Industrial Man* (Berkeley, CA: Gingko Press, 1951).

Codetta

1. See, for example, Kübler-Ross's memoir *The Wheel of Life: A Memoir of Living and Dying* (New York: Touchstone, 1997), where her end-of-life experiences with apparitions, spiritual figures, and ghosts clarified and extended her earlier work on the grief process.

2. Anne Anlin Cheng, "Skins, Tattoos, and Susceptibility," *Representations* 108, no. 1 (Fall 2009): 101.

Index

JAKE JOHNSON is an assistant professor of musicology at the University of Oklahoma. He is the author of *Lying in the Middle: Musical Theater and Belief at the Heart of America* and editor of *The Possibility Machine: Music and Myth in Las Vegas*.

The University of Illinois Press
is a founding member of the
Association of University Presses.

_____

Composed in 10.5/13 Mercury Text G1
with Avenir LT Std display
by Kirsten Dennison
at the University of Illinois Press

University of Illinois Press
1325 South Oak Street
Champaign, IL 61820-6903
www.press.uillinois.edu